TOUPIE LOWTHER

TOUPIE LOWTHER

Her life

VAL BROWN

"AB AMICIS SUIS COGNOSCENTIS EOS"

Copyright © 2017 Val Brown

The moral right of the author has been asserted.

Apart from any fair dealing for the purposes of research or private study, or criticism or review, as permitted under the Copyright, Designs and Patents Act 1988, this publication may only be reproduced, stored or transmitted, in any form or by any means, with the prior permission in writing of the publishers, or in the case of reprographic reproduction in accordance with the terms of licences issued by the Copyright Licensing Agency. Enquiries concerning reproduction outside those terms should be sent to the publishers.

Matador
9 Priory Business Park,
Wistow Road, Kibworth Beauchamp,
Leicestershire. LE8 0RX
Tel: 0116 279 2299
Email: books@troubador.co.uk
Web: www.troubador.co.uk/matador
Twitter: @matadorbooks

ISBN 978 1788035 231

British Library Cataloguing in Publication Data.
A catalogue record for this book is available from the British Library.

Printed and bound by CPI Group (UK) Ltd, Croydon, CR0 4YY
Typeset in 11pt Aldine401 BT by Troubador Publishing Ltd, Leicester, UK

Matador is an imprint of Troubador Publishing Ltd

Cover: The Lady Champions of England and France
Foils: Miss Toupie Lowther (England) and Madame Gabrièle (France)
"The Great Fencing Display 1902" by F H Townsend with grateful thanks
to Malcolm Fare and the National Fencing Museum

For Hilary

Contents

Introduction ix

1. Who was Toupie Lowther? 1
2. Francis William Lowther and Louise Beatrice de Fonblanque 5
3. Aimée Constance Anne Lowther 12
4. Claude William Henry Lowther 20
5. Education 31
6. Sporting Life: Fencing 37
7. Sporting Life: Tennis and Other Sports 47
8. The Batten Diaries 57
9. The Hacket Lowther Ambulance Unit 64
10. The Hackett Lowther Unit Goes To War 1918–1919 71
11. The Troubridge Diaries 83
12. A Few Other Friends 92
13. Fabienne Brethous-Lafargue 99
14. Music 109
15. Life, Death and her Will 113

Appendices
1. The Lowther Family 118
2. The Earl's Other Children 121
3. Aimée Lowther's Will 125
4. Les Ruches 130

5.	Fencing, Fiction, and Some Friends	133
6.	The Hillyard Family	138
7.	The German Spring Offensive of 1918 and more about the Hackett Lowther Ambulance Unit	142
8.	A Few Other People	154
9.	More Musical Compositions	160
10.	References – and Other Items of Interest	162
11.	"Le Salon de L'Amazone"	166

Sources and Thanks   168

Introduction

Toupie Lowther, the character behind that odd name and seemingly offensive persona who appears from time to time in the savage diary entries of Una Troubridge, has left very few of her own words. Now, however, when the researcher can look with ease through a century and more of newspaper reporting – *The Times* and *Sunday Times*, the *Daily Telegraph*, the *Express*, the *Sketch* and so on and so forth, even to the pages of the gossip columns of the *New York Times* – a new and intriguing personality emerges. The vast online stock of the British Newspaper Archives is full of entries – not long or complex, and not always overwhelmingly accurate – that report the latest deeds and doings of Miss Toupie Lowther. Even *The Motor Cycle* in 1919 cannot resist an entry that headlines A FAMOUS MOTOR CYCLIST: "Miss Toupie Lowther – who is a keen motorcyclist... and her companions are now demobilised", on her return from the Great War.

A few of her own words do survive in chapters written for other publications. From that mighty magazine *The Lady* in November 1899 describing her fencing career – and a handsomely written piece in his book *Forty Years of First Class Lawn Tennis* by Commander G. W. Hillyard. But of any personal diaries or letters no trace seems to remain. Or have yet been located. The grossly misguided identification of her by Michael Baker in his book *Our Three Selves*, as a Lady Barbara

Lowther, b. 1890, a daughter of the 6th Earl of Lonsdale and whose married name was Innes – effectively drowned Toupie's life and buried her achievements for many years.[1]

Sadly, most later writers seem to have allowed this sluggish identification to slide by unchallenged, although a glance at Debrett's *Peerage* might well have aroused some curiosity. It was not until Diana Souhami wrote her book, *The Trials of Radclyffe Hall* (Weidenfeld & Nicolson, 1998), that somebody successfully managed, in a couple of lines, to get it right.

Only one document written by Toupie in her own hand seems to have survived. Her report of the war service of the Hackett-Lowther Unit Motor Ambulance Section commanded by Sous-Lieutenant Victor Chatenay: Croix-de-Guerre, was written in 1920 and is currently held at the Imperial War Museum. There is also her Will – but this records her wishes at the end of her life, rather than her deeds during her higher days.

Toupie Lowther's successes as a woman athlete – fencer, tennis player, motorcyclist, motor-car driver – as well as her achievements as the founder of an ambulance unit in the War, and as a musician – whose family just happened to be on the fringes of Society (albeit with a rather delicate twist as to lineage) – made her a favourite with the Press, particularly in her younger days. This interest never quite went away, and can be said to be rooted not only in her deeds, but also in her particular type of character – a personality that chimed with adventure, daring, and talent. And a character who seems to have acquired in her lifetime (although known for a quick temper) an endless string, quota, queue and file of fine and lasting friends, who would quietly weep on the inside when she managed to lose a bout or a match that she should have won. A guess would be that she had very fine manners, and could rely upon that other gift of undeniable advantage – charm.

---

1 "Our Three Selves" by Michael Baker pub. Hamish Hamilton, 1985.

Introduction

To ensure the greatest accuracy possible, as well as searching newspaper and magazine press cuttings, this publication has made direct use of the UK Birth, Marriage, and Death records, will and probate records, baptismal records, UK naval, army and RAF records and naturalisation certificates, national census records and Debrett's *Peerage* 1951. Some Wikipedia entries deemed to be reliable have been quoted. Those which are more obviously dubious and/or manifestly incorrect have been avoided. Some records from some popular genealogical websites have been consulted, but not necessarily adopted. Where the author is not sure of certain information, a doubt will be expressed (for example, dubious nuggets from different newspapers around the world that laud exactly the same exploit whilst delicately employing varieties of language.

For any omissions that have been made by either ignorance or accident, sincere apologies are genuinely rendered.

I

WHO WAS TOUPIE LOWTHER?

May Lowther was born on 15th April 1874, the third child and second daughter of Lt Francis William Lowther, an officer in the Royal Navy, and his wife Louise Beatrice Lowther, née de Fonblanque, at their home in London, 7 Grafton Street.

She was always known as "Toupie", seemingly both in private as well as public, for reasons unknown and unguessable. Seemingly she was given no name other than the solitary May, although both her elder sister and brother were given three forenames. Why the baby of the family was stuck with just one name – and that one rejected by the bearer – remains a mystery.

As a child, most of her preliminary education would probably have been provided by a governess. An early fluency in the French language she later assigned to her mother's influence; Toupie is also credited as being well spoken in German. There's no reason to doubt this; her language skills were almost certainly polished by her boarding school. To this day still of historic high reputation and at that time situated in the town of Fontainbleau, near Paris. School was followed by some time at the Sorbonne in Paris, studying "En-Sciences" (see Chapter 5).

The effect, and thus the consequences, of the lazy misidentification by Michael Baker has been that any writer digging for details of Toupie's life before the arrival of the Internet has run into a blank wall. Sadly, Toupie has been widely described as a rather unpleasant, walk-on walk-off occasional side-player who materialises from time to time in the often plundered pages of Una Troubridge's diaries (featuring particularly during the rather heady 1920s and '30s, though with some slight asides of unspecified ambulance-driving service during the days of the Great War). Accounts of both her appearance and her personality have greatly suffered from what can only be described as a venom, deeply embedded in Lady Troubridge's pages, that seeped into the lesbian biographical literature of the 1970s and later.

Photo by W. Downey & Son Photographers, features in many sources, including the book Lawn Tennis at Home and Abroad *edited by Wallis Myers (New York, 1903). Possibly it was a family portrait: she seems to be about eighteen years old with the long hair "done-up" in a manner that would have been appropriate at the time.*

However, slipping this to one side, and looking afresh at other sources, Toupie Lowther can be seen to have made for herself a full and independent life. Sadly she wrote no diary, yet there are fragments of her life that remain visible, scattered around multiple newspaper clippings and in dusty pages of dusty books put together in times past. These narratives are now not difficult to locate, thanks to the digitalisation of newspapers, magazines, and the joys of the World Wide Web. From the new availability of long-forgotten books and the popular press, in both English and French, another very different woman gracefully emerges.

Who was Toupie Lowther?

At the beginning the twentieth century, a young Toupie Lowther was a sporting celebrity – widely and highly regarded in both Britain and France. Some references to her can even be found in American newspapers of the time. She competed regularly in the early years of of women's fencing, up to both competition and exhibition level: as well as in women's local and international championship lawn tennis. Although by no means always a winner, as a young woman the press reporters of the time seem to have loved her: she was frequently interviewed, often quoted, and from time to time called upon to contribute instructive articles to smart women's magazines.

Her life seems to have been always full of activity, from the high-style exhibition thrust of the foil at home and the thwack of the ball across the net into the near and far borders of European tennis – up to her service in France under fire and gas during the latter days of the War. In her later years she seems to have taken up the perhaps lesser thud of the golf ball, and became known as a fine piano player and composer. She is described as having a good singing voice. A number of her published compositions for voice and piano survive in libraries around the world, though very likely, nowadays, not often publicly performed.

Throughout her life she chose to use the name Toupie. So far the reason behind this choice of nickname is not clear: "Toupie" is French for "top" or "spindle". However, this was her chosen form of address and the name by which she was always known to her family, her friends and the Press, and it was her signature on formal documents. Possibly because she resembled an energetic spinning top as a small child, or, as in "Tippi" Hedren (the star of Hitchcock's film *The Birds*) a term of endearment for a small girl deriving from Swedish or Hebrew.

Interestingly Toupie Lowther has also slipped into fiction. She appears briefly in *Murder in Montparnasse*[1] – *A Phryne Fisher*

---

1   One of a series of murder mysteries now dramatised for television.

Mystery by the Australian detective writer Kerry Greenwood, alongside a fictional Dolly Wilde and a smattering of snapshot quotes from the pen of Natalie Barney. Toupie also makes an appearance in a walk-on role as Mrs Pankhurst's driver in the graphic novel *Suffrajitsu*[2] and features again, but more prominently, in two American Foreworld Saga novellae: *The Pale Blue Ribbon* by John Longenbaugh and *The Isle of Dogs* by Michael Lussier. At the time of writing, these two novellae are only available on the Internet.

*Egerton Mansions, London SW.
Her home for many years.*

---

2   *Suffrajitsu: Mrs Pankhurst's Amazons*, written by Tony Wolf and illustrated by Joao Vieira. Available in hard copy and also online in the UK. See Appendix 5.

2

FRANCIS WILLIAM LOWTHER AND LOUISE BEATRICE DE FONBLANQUE

The Lowther Family

Toupie's father, Francis William Lowther, was an illegitimate son of William, Viscount Lowther, who, after a diplomatic career in Europe would become the 2nd Earl of Lonsdale in 1844.[3] Francis William was born in Genoa, also known as Genova, in the (then) Kingdom of Sardinia: records show that he was baptised on 24th February at the Genoa British Chaplaincy. He became a full British citizen in April 1865 – his application for citizenship supported by his father, as well as by Henry Lowther, the MP for West Cumberland (later to be the 3rd Earl of Lonsdale); along with George Augustus Frederick Cavendish-Bentinck MP (who was married to a sister of the 2nd Earl); and the Hon. Henry William Stanhope. With this line-up of honourable gentlemen to hand, clearly no life problems would have been anticipated or, indeed, encountered.

---

3   The 2nd Earl of the second creation. There is a fine portrait of the 2nd Earl as a young man on display in the National Portrait Gallery in London.

5

Francis William's mother is named in his father's will as an *Emilia Cresotti*; she has been identified by some sources as an opera singer, and this may well be so. There are several glancing references which mention an Adelaide Cressotti, or Creossotti,[4] as either a contralto or mezzo-soprano opera singer of the early 1800s. She sang in Lisbon but seems also to have performed in Genoa.

The young Francis William came to London as a small child in 1846 and lived with his father in the handsome Lonsdale town house at 14/15 Carlton Terrace in Westminster. Growing up and, as an illegitimate son, needing a career of his own, he chose to enter the Royal Navy, and entered the service as an officer cadet in 1856. A midshipman, he served on HMS Pique during the Second China War of 1856–60, and alongside all the crew was decorated with the China Medal. Commissioned as a lieutenant in 1861, his naval records have survived in the National Archives at Kew.

In 1868, the then Lt Francis William Lowther, a serving Naval officer and now a naturalised British subject , grandly married Miss Louise Beatrice de Fonblanque, the 21-year-old daughter of Edward Barrington de Fonblanque[5] and his Canadian wife, Lavinia Mary Foot(e).

The young couple were married on Wednesday, 29th April

St James Church.
With thanks to Fran Pickering.

---

4   *Changing the Score* by Hilary Poriss (Oxford University Press, 2009) inter alia.
5   Writer, traveller, historian and renowned man of Letters: 1820–1895.

at St James's Church, Piccadilly, London, still handsomely standing today – a Wren church with highly esteemed internal decoration by Grinling Gibbons. The bride's parents were present alongside a distinguished and elegant company of guests, some family, some titled, some parliamentary, and without doubt many other friends. It was clearly a grand wedding in a fine church with a full congregation. Rather strangely *The Times* seems not to have remarked on the happy occasion, but other newspapers certainly did. No doubt to cheers and noisy best wishes from all present, a very noble reception at 14/15 Carlton Terrace followed.

At last the happy couple left London to honeymoon for a few days in Paris, and from thence to a longer stay in the Isle of Wight before the groom went back to his work and duty. Interestingly, among the guests were Frances Broadwood,[6] the groom's (half) sister, her husband, Henry Broadwood, and one of their two sons.[7] After a banquet-style wedding breakfast and sumptuous entertainments with a glittering array of wealthy, titled and fashionable socialites at Carlton House Terrace, the couple honeymooned in Paris and then spent several weeks at Thornton House, Puckpool, the Isle of Wight residence of Captain Marcus Lowther, RN[8]. At the time Francis Lowther was Flag Lieutenant to Vice-Admiral Sir Baldwin Walker KCB, Commander-in-Chief of The Nore [an area of the Medway in Kent] based at Sheerness.[9]

---

6 Née Lowther. See Appendix 2.
7 British Newspaper Archive: *The Yorkshire Post and Leeds Intelligencer* 2nd May 1868.
8 Marcus Lowther (1820–1908) was a notable member of the extended Lowther family; he was also a professional naval officer and gained the rank of Rear Admiral.
9 Contribution above with thanks to Hastings Press. The Nore, a sandbank where the River Thames meets the North Sea, was a major anchorage for the Navy's North Sea Fleet. A smaller anchorage, Little Nore, was near Sheerness. A naval command had been established there in 1752 and was responsible for sub-commands at Chatham, Sheerness, Harwich and Humber.

The couple's first child, a daughter, followed swiftly in 1869. Born in Sheerness she was named Aimée Constance Anne. Their second child, a son, was named Claude William Henry: he arrived in 1871 when the family was living in Binstead on the Isle of Wight.

In 1872, after the death of his father and now holding the rank of Commander, Francis William Lowther retired from active service, although he continued to serve, and, as was usual, attract promotion, in the Royal Navy Reserve. Generously remembered in his father's will, Francis William received the benefit of a very handsome trust fund worth about £124,000, alongside considerable incomes from other additional rents and mortgages.

The couple's third child and second daughter, named May, but always known as "Toupie", was born on 15th April 1874 at 7, Grafton Street, Westminster, the then family home in London. The growing family seems to have necessitated a move, and the Lowthers then moved to, and lived, quite grandly, at 73 Pont Street in Chelsea, London for some time.

Clearly not a man who espoused idleness, Cmdr Francis William Lowther began a successful second career as a man of business. He was a partner in Punchard, McTaggart, Lowther and Co., a company with a penchant for selling stock in the newly emerging railway companies and which branched out to become what seems to have been a very successful naval engineering business, both abroad and in the UK. Cmdr Lowther was obviously a man whose choice in life was to work. A man who would get up in the morning, have his breakfast, and then go off to a full day at the office and elsewhere, rather than one who would choose to stay leisurely at home.

In 1876 he was advanced to the naval rank of Retired Captain, and was only removed from the Navy List in 1908 at his death.[10] Captain Lowther died in London on 30th March at 13 Upper

---

10   In Naval records terminology, he "Failed to report for duty".

Brook Street, Grosvenor Square. He had been in poor health for some time, having lost the use of his legs and been confined to a wheelchair for many years. His death certificate indicates the cause of death as: "Paraplegia cystitis 17 years: Consecutive nephritis: Asthenia syncope:" a prolonged heart condition. The certificate is signed by Henry Gwynne Lawrence MD.

A memorial service for Francis William Lowther was held at St Paul's Church in Knightsbridge on 6th April: attended by his widow Louise, with their two daughters, Aimée and Toupie. And with no doubt many other mourners. On the same day his son, Claude, in a private ceremony for family only, placed an urn containing his father's ashes upon the tomb of the 2nd Earl of Lonsdale at the Lowther mausoleum in Cumbria.[11]

Generous obituaries describe his personality:

"... a gentleman of charming personality, old world courtliness, and great intellect he was revered by all who had the honour of his friendship... his grip on the affairs of the day and the trend of modern life was amazing when one reflects that for fifteen years he had been paralysed from the waist and unable to leave his chair...a gracious and kindly gentleman."

The *New York Times* said it well, and included his daughters: "London April 4th – The West End of London has lost one its most favorite [sic] figures in the death of Capt. Lowther whose wit was as light as his infirmities were heavy. His bath chair in Hyde Park was daily surrounded by a crowd of persons of social eminence. Capt. Lowther leaves two daughters, both women of prominence, Aimée Lowther being a noted amateur actress, while her sister is one of the finest fencers of the day as well as a good tennis player and an intrepid motorist."[12]

In his will Francis William Lowther left his business interests to his son, and also put money aside for a trust fund

---
11 Ref: inter alia the *Carlisle Patriot*, 10th April 1908.
12 *New York Times*, 5th April 1908.

to be set up to provide an income for his wife and daughters: one half going to his wife and the remaining half to be divided equally between his two daughters. He directed also that upon their deaths each portion of the trust should devolve to the remaining survivors – as the last surviving member of his family, after Aimée's death in 1935, Toupie would have had a very substantial income.[13]

Louise Beatrice de Fonblanque was born in Toronto, Canada. She was the eldest child of Edward Barrington de Fonblanque, a distinguished travel writer, scholar and traveller, and his wife Lavinia Maria (or Mary) Foot(e). Edward Barrington de Fonblanque was a grandson of John Anthony de Fonblanque, the distinguished lawyer and MP.[14]

They were married in the Anglican Christ Church Cathedral, Montreal on 22nd July 1843 and Louise was born on 4th October 1846 in Toronto, the couple's first child, and was baptised on 13th December at St James's Cathedral in the city. A sister, Constance Barrington de Fonblanque, was also born in Canada. A third sister, also Lavinia Mary, and a son, Lester Ramsay de Fonblanque, the only brother, were born in England and there are many descendants living today.[15]

Mrs Francis Lowther, one of a set by Julia Margaret Cameron (1815–79).

Throughout her marriage Louise Beatrice was always referred to, properly at the time, as Mrs Francis Lowther. As a young woman she was photographed in a series of portraits by Julia Cameron, great aunt to the writer Virginia Woolf; no other photographs of her seem to have survived.

A portrait of Mrs Francis Lowther by the artist Ellen Montalba is mentioned as being

---

13 Ref. BMD and his will. The Newspaper Archive online.
14 A French protestant he was also entitled to use his title of Marquis, but seems to have declined to do so.
15 Many thanks to Paula Searle and her contribution to this chapter.

exhibited at the Royal Academy in the *Art Journal* of July 1873, although its current whereabouts is unknown. However, there seems to have been another portrait of Mrs Francis Lowther, painted by the great George Frederic Watts, which was sold at Sotheby's in 1891. The portrait may still be in private hands but it can be seen frequently reproduced online.

Widowed in 1908, Louise Beatrice, Mrs. Francis Lowther, seems to have continued to live at 51 Sloane Street in London. However, she died at St Aubyns Mansions, Hove, on the 6th September 1922 – a fine late Victorian block of apartments facing the busy sea and beachy seaside in Hove near Brighton. Some sources indicate that she owned one of the apartments, number 7, although in the street directories of the time she does not appear as a permanent resident.

St Aubyns Mansions, photo by the writer, 2016.

The death certificate describes Toupie as the "informant" and "present at the death". In her will Mrs Francis Lowther asks her medical attendant that after her death "he shall remove my heart or otherwise completely convince himself that life is extinct and then my body shall be cremated and the ashes thrown to the winds". The wills of both her daughters contain a similar instruction to a doctor or medical attendant.

Her body was indeed cremated, and sources say that the ashes were removed to Herstmonceux Castle by her son Claude, where, most properly, and most certainly, any wishes would have been carried out.[16]

---

16 Birth certificates, marriage certificates, death certificates from UK BMD. The wills of Francis William Lowther and Louise Beatrice Lowther, the *London Gazette*.

3

AIMÉE CONSTANCE ANNE LOWTHER

Aimée Constance Anne Lowther, Toupie's older sister, was born on 16th February 1869 at Kent House, Mile Town, Sheerness on the Isle of Sheppey where her father was serving as the Flag Lieutenant to Vice Admiral Sir Baldwin Walker, then Commander-in-Chief of the Nore Command.[17] She died on 4th February 1935 at her home in 10 Montpelier Crescent in Brighton – now divided into flats. The cause of death is given as tuberculosis and the death certificate is signed by Dr Octavia Wilberforce, whose surgery was also in Montpelier Crescent.[18]

As with most young women of a certain class and background, in May 1888, aged nineteen, and alongside the usual multitude of young women from new and old noble families (and if not so noble then very wealthy), Aimée was presented to the Queen at what was known as a "Drawing-Room", and so officially "came out" into Society.[19] This was shorthand of the time (and even today) as now being grown

---

17 See Chapter 2.
18 For those interested in the lives of early women doctors, read *Octavia Wilberforce* by Pat Jalland (Cassell, 1989).
19 *The Times* report of the ceremony states that Aimée was presented to the Queen by her mother.

up and available for marriage. Interestingly, but probably not surprisingly, there is no similar report in *The Times* that her younger sister Toupie was ever presented to the Queen in the same tradition and manner. Of course, at nineteen years old, Toupie was already in stockings and knickerbockers with a mask over her face and a foil dancing in her hand. The Queen, probably, would not have been impressed.

Few life-facts about the sixty-six years of Aimée's life have survived. However a few interesting snippets from her younger years can be uncovered from the pages of the nationwide newspaper archives: gossip, artistic reviews, and references to some of her friends. These cuttings mainly describe her interests and appearances in staged "dramatic productions". Many newspaper sources hintingly praise her as a fine "amateur actress" and, invariably, as though scratching around for something else to say, go on to mention that she was a close friend of the actress Ellen Terry, and that she had received an invitation to the coronation ceremony of King Edward VII. Swiftly followed by additional information that she "is the sister of the well-known sportswoman Miss Toupée Lowther [sic]".

Aimée Lowther looking ahead, with Ellen Terry to her left. Photograph from The Tatler, *March 1906 titled "Before the Curtain".*

In one of Ellen Terry's biographies a piece is included that the actress hails as: "The following delightful 'skit'… suggested itself to my clever friend Miss Aimée Lowther", which goes on to include a false nose, an errant grand-daughter and a vigorous kick being humorously landed on an over-keen reporter. It is clever, and nicely written.[20]

---

20 *The Story of My Life* by Ellen Terry with Illustrations (Hutchinson & Co., 1908).

Aimée Lowther as Pierrot in Dream Flower: *from The Sketch 5th April 1899: original photographer unknown.*

Aimée seems not to have ever been attracted to a more permanent professional stage career, but from time to time she clearly enjoyed featuring in the semi-spotlight as an amateur performer – and even occasionally in breeches – mostly artistic achievements, rather than dramatic presentations. In particular, the production and performance of the popular "tableau vivant" genre: a favourite staging for high-class charity performances by both professional and amateur "celebrities" who would, most likely, enjoy posing in fine costumes and gliding around beautifully with both charm and grace.

Her on-stage appearances in *The Pierrot of the Minute*: A Dramatic Fantasy in One Act written by Ernest Dowson[21] (with incidental music by Miss Toupie Lowther") and *The Dream Flower* (a musical comedy, a charming "play without words" by Aimée Lowther, with music by Mrs Lyndoch Moncrieff), in 1888 and 1889, were warmly praised by the critics. However, history seems not to have retained any solid description, or indeed indication, of the dramatic action. This, if any, would probably have been largely dance and mime, along with fine costumes. Later performances seem to have used freshly composed incidental music.

The Times also wrote of Aimée's performances in *Engaged*, a play by W. S. Gilbert in 1898, with music by Ralph Barnham. There was also a dip into the historic past with a "moral masque" (by Thomas Dekker and John Ford, first

---

21   Ernest Christopher Dowson (1867–1900). *Pierrot of the Minute* is also a "Comedy Overture" composed by Sir Granville Bantock in 1909.

published in 1656) titled *The Sun's Darling* in November 1906 at Queen's Gate Hall. There is every reason to suppose that her stagecraft was both graceful and gracious, popular and well received by her audiences.

A story, frequently cited and variably presented (and thus its origin and originality is unfathomable), involves a brush with Oscar Wilde. He is reputed to have gallantly said: "Aimée, si vous aviez én garcon, vous auriez gâché ma vie."[22] There is little reason to doubt that, along with her sister (and indeed her brother), Aimée Lowther had a wide acquaintance with the artistic and literary talents of the "fin de siècle". Which would certainly have included Oscar Wilde.

She is said to have been fluent in French, as was her sister Toupie, and it would be most likely that she too was taught to speak French as a child by their mother.

Aimée Lowther on stage: performance and photographer unknown.

Aimée would be best described as a woman of artistry: of poetry and of the stage but never in a professional sense. Neither the publicity of the competitive sporting life, nor the public turbulence and demands of a political calling – which surrounded both her younger sister and brother – seem to have held any attraction for her. Yet she was clearly not in awe of, or frightened by, performing to an audience. A family trait shared by all three siblings.

A will from 1930, and a sequel with codicils dated just before she died in 1935 are readily available indicators of her life and personality. They portray

---

22 "Aimée, if you had been a boy you would have ruined my life."

a woman of forceful character and firm opinion who moved alongside both the professional theatrical personalities as well as being a major player in the titled and untitled amateurly artistic classes. All enjoying a considerable degree of public appreciation and well supplied with adequate financial resources. As was the young Aimée Lowther.

Possibly not dramatically talented to a professional level – the Lowther family seems not, in its long history, to have produced many individuals who were drawn to dabbling in cultural and artistic matters – she did however find her métier in later life. Aimée became a dedicated, rampant even, fine art and antiques gatherer, collector, and hoarder.

She bequeathed three items to the Victoria and Albert Museum: "my antique silver basin and ewer and seventeenth century German red glass tankard (formerly in the possession of the late Col. Claude Lowther)". These were indeed sent to the V&A by her executors on 23rd July 1935, but the silver basin and ewer were turned down by the museum – and were returned. The red glass tankard, however, was accepted, and is on display to this day.

Her house at 10 Montpelier Crescent, Brighton seems to have slipped into becoming an immense depositary of aesthetic, elegant, refined and desirable objects of culture and fine taste. From the pages of her will(s) it is clear that her home was brimful with paintings, books, tapestries, fine china, plate, silver, glass and clocks, all on display or stored in cupboards. There was antique walnut and mahogany furniture, and pictures aplenty in oil, watercolour and pastel. There were cabinets, bookcases, chests of drawers, trunks, all stacked full: the overflow was safely stored at Messrs Arding and Hobbs in Clapham Junction, South London, and with the National Provincial bank. There were also portfolios of scrapbooks and photographs in antique boxes and leather cases.[23]

---

23 See Appendix 3.

Toupie was a major beneficiary of Aimée's will, as well as an executor (along with the solicitor), and became, inter alia, the inheritor of the contents of all the cupboards, bookcases, chests of drawers, etc., together with a set of lapis-handled dinner knives, a crested plated tea tray, all Aimée's pewter articles and first choice of books and linen. Plus the marble statue of a child on a marble base (in store at Arding and Hobbs) ascribed to Bouchardon, and (interestingly) "all my literary works in a large leather portfolio and in a bound manuscript covered with silk together with papers, photographs, portfolios..."[24] Toupie also became the happy owner of the iron gates which once grandly fronted Claude Lowther's house in Catherine Street in London, as well as an iron candelabra from Herstmonceux Castle.

Aimée directed that "the marble statue of the Weeping Child which belonged to [her] late brother Col. Claude Lowther shall be placed on a bracket over his memorial tablet in Hurstmonceux [sic] church, Sussex". Sadly, the marble statue was either not put in place, or has since, rather unsurprisingly, vanished.

She was generous with her fortune in death and did not cease from afflicting terms, directions, orders and conditions to her legacies – and presumably burdens to her executors. Clearly a woman of both philanthropy and a firm determination, Aimée insisted that her wishes be carried out to the letter. There were to be no short-cuts or assumptions by her executors to save time, and her beneficiaries were to be suitably and duly satisfied exactly as she so desired.

Aimée continued with her directions concerning her body after death – a small legacy was left to the doctor who would wield the knife:

"After the brain is removed or the heart is pierced... and on no account buried. I am quite indifferent as to what

---

24 If her own, which could well be so, presumably unpublished. Or possibly the reference is to other book collections.

happens to the ashes but I especially desire that no lid be placed over my coffin after the veins have been cut on the fifth day..."

A similar paragraph can be found in the wills of her mother and of Toupie. They indicate membership of – or at least sympathy with – the Victorian embrace of the aims and objectives described in "The Society for the Prevention of Premature Burial."[25]

The two unnamed contributors to Aimée Lowther's obituary, which appeared in *The Times* of 12th February 1935, are probably well suited to describe her personality.

"H.S." portrays her as

"... a notable individualist... [with] innate appreciation of the period of the grand seigneur... aesthetically refined, she also collected an exclusive circle of friends. Not obviously generous, she did her charitable duties in her own manner."

"A Friend" writes:

"... her genius was for conversation, and its distinctive trait was intellectual vitality... her taste in literature on the whole was for French writers – especially for masters of form like Anatole France... perhaps she would not suffer fools very gladly... [but] also disliked affectation and pretension."

Just like her sister and brother, Aimée Lowther did not marry. So far, no known lovers have been either uncovered or identified.

---

25 By William Tebb: "With special reference to trance, catalepsy, and other forms of suspended animation" (Swann Sonnenschein & Co. Ltd, 1905). Available to read on the Internet Archive.

Aimée Constance Anne Lowther

10 & 11 Montpelier Crescent today.

4

CLAUDE WILLIAM HENRY LOWTHER

Claude William Henry Lowther, Toupie's older brother, was the second child of the family. The solitary son he was born in 1870 in Binstead on the Isle of Wight when his father was a serving Naval officer. He died at his London home, 43 Catherine Street, Westminster, on 17th June 1929. Two photographs of him by Sir (John) Benjamin Stone are in the collections of the National Portrait Gallery.

Claude's childhood seems to have been routine for such a class of family at that time. He went away to prep school as a child, and from thence to Rugby School, although his time there seems not to have been too long.

Upon leaving school there appears to be no evidence of any time of further study at either Oxford or Cambridge, and as a young man with no particular ambition (or need to work), he seems to have led a life not dissimilar to that of most energetic and thoughtless young men from a well-heeled, well-placed background. Two adventures which made it into several newspapers in the early 1890s involved his appearance at two separate magistrates' courts. At Bow Street Court, alongside three other young men, he was charged with assaulting two police officers after an incident at a box in a Covent Garden

Theatre fancy dress ball. This involved "a dummy dressed up as an elderly gentleman" which ended up at a lower level in the stalls. And he appeared before Marlborough Street Police Courts after he had been arrested for illegally driving a horse-drawn hansom cab. Seemingly he had said, "It's all right bobby – it's only a lark you know. I asked the cabman to let me drive for a while." At the hearing itself he described himself as "of no occupation".[26]

Both episodes are typical of the behaviour of wealthy young men without work or study to occupy their time. His father, however, would not have been at all pleased, and no doubt his mother was equally distressed at the publicity, let alone the offences. Unsurprisingly, therefore, on 14th March 1894 there was a report in *The Times* of a golden opportunity, guaranteed to extract Claude from the temptations of the London night-life – that was always open to a young man with nothing much else to do – and an opening to what could be carved into a handsome career:

"Mr Claude Lowther was presented at court on appointment as hon. attaché in HM Diplomatic service by Rt Hon. James Lowther, MP."

Claude Lowther was then found a post at the British Embassy in Madrid, under the Ambassador of the time, Sir Henry Drummond Wolff. [27]

The Rt Honourable James William Lowther, an influential and well-respected MP and later holder of the post of Speaker of the House of Commons from 1905 to 1921, was, of course, a family relative. Many generations of the men of the Lowther family had followed lifelong and successful careers in the foreign diplomatic service, in Europe and worldwide. It would not be hard to guess that the young Claude's father had had

---

26 Inter alia the *Derby Daily* and the *Hull Daily Mail*, 8th July 1891, and the *Aberdeen Evening Express* 11th February 1892. This second episode seems to have been widely reported.
27 See appendix 8.

some hand in securing this fine diplomatic appointment for his – possibly becoming wayward – son.

There was diplomatic history on both sides of the family. Claude's maternal grandfather, Edward Barrington de Fonblanque (1821–95) had been a worldwide globe-trotter and traveller, a distinguished author and frequent commissioner and emissary for the British Government. However, there is no reason to suppose that this sudden Spanish "opportunity" was greeted with open arms by the young man. It would, of course, involve actual desk work: office hours, mandatory discipline and (most likely) dull diplomatic dinners. All in a foreign land where he would no doubt be required to master the Spanish language.

And indeed, his time in Madrid was short lived. Two years later Claude's request to leave his post as attaché to the British Embassy in Madrid, dated 22nd August 1896, is recorded in the archives of the British Foreign Office.

Upon his return home, a swift entry into the Westmorland and Cumberland Yeomanry was followed by an upgrade into the (junior) officer ranks of the recently formed Imperial Yeomanry: a "volunteer" rather than professional cavalry regiment created on 24th December 1899. With South Africa and the Boers particularly in mind. During the 2nd Boer War (1899–1902) Claude served as a lieutenant with the 24th company, 8th battalion, becoming eligible for the award of the Queens South African medal for Campaign service, without clasp.[28]

There are some references that he was also unsuccessfully recommended for the award of the Victoria Cross for his service. However, there appears to be no extant or official confirmation of this, nor description of any qualifying episode.

There is no reason to suppose that a full-time career in the army, any more than a diplomatic career overseas, ever

---

28 *The Times* 20th June 1899, the *Whitstable Times* and the *Herne Bay Herald* 20th October 1900, *inter alia*.

attracted any permanent ambition. Possibly the short clerical sojourn in Madrid, swiftly followed by a commission into the army and a few months with horse and rifle chasing the Boers, was, in fact, a long-term plan to qualify Claude Lowther for a more distinguished – and even lifelong – handsome career at home. A career which would require actual work for no more than six months of the year. Upon returning home from South Africa, and by the turn of the century, he was very smartly heading for that other path greatly favoured by generations of Lowther sons: winning a seat and entering Parliament as an MP. And, very likely, not without some supportive help from relatives and/or other family friends – Hugh Lowther, the 5th Earl of Lonsdale for example, as well as from the Rt Hon. James Lowther MP, steadily building his career as the longest-serving Speaker in the House of Commons.

All went well. By December 1900 Claude William Henry Lowther had been successfully elected as the Liberal Unionist MP for Eskdale in North Cumberland, a constituency which, unsurprisingly, included part of the Lonsdale estate, and where the Lowther name could almost certainly attract a workable majority of votes. He chose to make his home in nearby handsome and historic Scaleby Castle, a fine building with a Pele tower and a one-time double moat. The castle is still standing.

Claude William Henry Lowther MP by Sir (John) Benjamin Stone, NPG 31530. Reproduced with permission from the NPG.

Unfortunately in the 1906 election he lost his seat, but managed to be re-elected in 1910. In the 1918 election he stood again: since the constituency of Eskdale had been abolished, Claude William Henry was returned as a

Coalition Unionist MP for the constituency of Lonsdale in North Lancashire.

Scaleby Castle, thanks to an unknown photographer.

His time as an MP was always volatile. Most likely due to continuing poor health he finally chose not to stand in the 1922 election. In his parliamentary career, Claude Lowther is mostly remembered for involving himself in an association with the Anti-Socialist Union: supporting free trade, opposing the spread of socialism, and participating in the activities of the ultra-conservative Primrose League. A dramatic speaker, his rhetoric could charm an audience. As a flavour of his high-Tory views, when engaging a prospective Labour candidate in a debate on "Will Socialism Benefit the People", he told a packed audience that socialism "would confiscate everybody's wealth", giving "no more to Marconi than to his least intelligent worker". He drew "loud applause" for affirming that "our cities" were "flooded with the alien scum of the earth", "sweated alien goods should be kept out", and that the Poor Law "bred paupers".[29]

Socially he acquired a wide circle around him of prominent men and women of the time – the wealthy, the artistic and the political – and was known for fine, not to say exquisite tailoring. A modern-day description renders him thus: "Tall and handsome, insouciant but courteous", with a penchant for "magnificent waistcoats with evening attire… a black velvet cape with scarlet lining… with an antique top hat".[30]

It was in the early days of his years as an MP that he made an attempt towards a theatrical sideline. On 21st May 1903 at

---

29 The *Carlisle Patriot*, quoted from "Claude Lowther, MP (1870–1929). "Wit, Tragedy, Melodrama and mystery in Public Life", by A. N. Connell, Appleby-in-Westmorland, as yet unpublished.

30 Thanks to A. N. Connell 2016.

His Majesty's Theatre in London, Claude William Henry's (probably) only stab at playwriting hit the boards. Named *The Gordian Knot*, produced by Mr Herbert Beerbohm Tree and starring Miss Olga Nethersole. The play lasted only a few performances, so scathing and savage were the reviews. Historically the play is said to have been one of London's most spectacular failures. Regretfully it would seem that any original script has been, mysteriously, banished to oblivion. All that remains are the prompt books, held at Bristol University.

During his years as an MP, Claude Lowther gained no parliamentary office. Some snippets of his speeches do survive, however, and are described as both controversial and witty.

Herstmonceux Castle, from "The King's England, Sussex" by Arthur Mee. pub. 1938.[31]

Claude William Henry moved his home away from Cumberland in the north to East Sussex in the south, where, if anywhere, he is still remembered. In 1911 he acquired the then crumbling and moatless (but still gracious) Hurstmonceux Castle – now renamed "Herstmonceux" for some no doubt local reason –

---

31   Photographer unknown: published with thanks to Messrs. Hodder & Stoughton. The castle was clearly photographed before any restoration had taken place. The magazine *Country Life* also visited Herstmonceux Castle in 1918 for its series "Country Homes and Gardens Old & New", the reporter was Martin Conway. Frances Garnet, Lady Wolseley, also visited the Castle in 1928 for *The Sussex County Magazine*.

and put himself to the task of rehabilitation, renovation and restoration of a very stately, and still just about habitable, ruin.

The arrival of war in 1914 brought Claude an opportunity to try for another dip into army life, that other highly-favoured career for so many of the sons of Lowther. Still holding his seat as MP for Eskdale, having already involved himself as the Hon Lieutenant in the assembling of a local Home Defence Force at Herstmonceux, a fine appeal for volunteers to join the Royal Sussex Regiment was headlined in the *Eastbourne Gazette* on 9th September 1914:

"ANOTHER BATTALION OF SUSSEX INFANTRY: TO BE RAISED BY MR CLAUDE LOWTHER MP

"With the sanction of Lord Kitchener, Mr Claude Lowther MP (Herstmonceux Castle) is raising another battalion of Infantry which he will command and will accompany where ever it goes."

Claude William Henry was appointed to the command of the 1st Southdown Battalion – later the 11th (Service) Battalion – Royal Sussex Regiment on 1st September 1914. His commission as Temporary Lieutenant Colonel was gazetted on 14th October 1914. Two other Southdown (service) Battalions of the Royal Sussex followed: the 2nd and the 3rd, later becoming the 12th and the 13th.

A year later, however, on 2nd September 1915, Claude William Henry relinquished his commission, having been "requested to do so" because of ill health. So he did not go to France with the 11th Southdown Battalion – to become known as "Lowther's Lambs" – in 1916. He was not then entitled to the War Service medals, which were issued to all service ranks in 1919 – both men and women – who had served abroad during the war. Nor, it would seem, did any other post-war civilian decoration to honour even his initial effort in raising the Southdown Battalions, ever come his way.[32]

The 11th, 12th and 13th (Service) Battalions of the Royal Sussex Regiment served on 30th June 1916 at the Battle of the Boar's Head, to great losses.

The 11th (Service) Battalion of the Border Regiment Cumberland and Westmorland, was raised by Hugh Lowther, the 5th Earl of Lonsdale and known as "The Lonsdales". The battalion served on the first day of the Battle of the Somme, 1st July 1916, also to great losses. "The Lonsdales" was also a "Pals" battalion.[33]

Claude Lowther was born to achieve a distinguished life and to follow a successful career. Preparatory school, public school, diplomatic service, the army, Parliamentary service and a multitude of influential relatives – his life's profile indicated that he would become a man of action and drive. A man who had the background and the means to fulfil, with style, any aspiration or ambition that he might nourish.

He was a rich man throughout his life, becoming and being known as a collector

Claude Lowther as an MP.
From Punch,
12th April 1905.

---

32 Lt Colonel Lowther's service records are held at the National Archives. The three Southdown Battalions were recruited from the many rural and county towns of the Downs, all founded on the "Pals Battalions" principle: men living close to each other in the same village or street – who enlisted together, trained together, and went on to fight together. And indeed then died together, often leaving families, streets and villages with no sons surviving.
33 The Cumbria Museum of Military Life, the archives of the *Bexhill Observer* and many other websites.

of fine art and antiques, no doubt to shine inside his home, Herstmonceux Castle. Indeed, his estate upon his death was valued in six figures. But this undoubted wealth had mostly been inherited, and his life seems to have gained no particularly riveting plaudits for either academic, artistic, diplomatic, parliamentary, or, any lasting historical deed. As an MP he gained neither public honour nor ministerial office. Most of his alterations to Herstmonceux Castle have been replaced by later owners: he remains largely a forgotten man. Except, perhaps, in East Sussex and some long memories of the Royal Sussex Regiment Southdown Battalions who served and fell in the Great War.[34]

In his will there are listed, inter alia, items such as a seventeenth-century Dantzig Rose bowl, a tortoiseshell cigarette case with a crest in diamonds, diamond cuff links, a ruby heart with a cross, four Sheffield plate candlesticks, and a silver-gilt Elizabethan centre piece (bequeathed to him by his father). Also itemised are an eighteenth-century picture in a gold oval frame, subject "Head of a Woman" attributed to Drouis (*sic:* probably Drouais) and a seventeenth-century picture in a gold and glass frame attributed to Canaletto. There are also clothes, waistcoat buttons, brushes, and more cuff links. His death certificate indicates "1a: Hypocardial degeneration of heart: b: cirrhosis of liver: 2. chronic morphinism (twenty years standing)." The death was certified by Claude William Henry's neighbour, Dr A. Dumas Child, whose address is given as 49 Catherine Street, SW1.[35]

His sister Aimée is not remembered in his will; all Toupie gets is the Louis XVI bed which had once belonged to their mother. The bed had originally been bequeathed to Claude William Henry in her will.

---

34 *The Times*, Obit d. 18th June 1929.
35 Dr A. Dumas Child also attended Marguerite Radclyffe Hall in her final days. Most likely he was the Dr Armando Dumas Child who is named as the actress Vivien Leigh's doctor at the time of her death.

Claude William Henry Lowther

A memorial service was held on Saturday, 30th June 1929 at "All Saints" the Herstmonceux Parish Church. At Herstmonceux Castle, in the room which was once the chapel, there is a commemorative plaque on the wall, where his ashes are placed.

Claude William Henry Lowther, along with his sisters, did not marry. However, he may have had at least one natural son, Claude Michael John Barrington, who was born *c.* 1896 (see Appendix 8).

His sisters placed a fine plaque to their brother's memory in All Saints' Church in the village of Herstmonceux. The church is situated about two miles east of the village centre along the A271, and is then approached from the north through Flowers Green.

"This tablet is erected to the memory of Lt Colonel Claude William Henry Lowther by his two sisters."

He was Lord of the Manor of Hurstmonceux until 19th June 1929 when he died aged fifty-seven. He partly restored Hurstmonceux Castle which he found in a ruin and left in a monument of beauty. He served in the Boer War in 1899 and was recommended for conspicuous gallantry. He was Conservative M.P. for North Cumberland from 1910 to 1918 and afterwards for the Lonsdale division of Lancashire until 1922. At the outbreak of the war in 1914 he raised and equipped five Battalions of the Royal Sussex Regiment known as Lowther's Lambs. He was a man of many gifts with an inspired and poetical sense of beauty. A generous master and a witty companion. His memory will linger in some hearts."

5

EDUCATION

Henry de Goudourville, in his twin-volume *Escrimeurs Contemporains*[36] published in 1899, presents tomes of biographical homage to the prominent European gentlemen fencers of his time. He also included a page and a half describing Miss Toupie Lowther. In his two heavy volumes, she is the only woman included.

It is M. de Goudourville who makes a reference to Toupie's schooling – that she attended "Le Pensionnat Les Ruches" in the commune of Avon, near Fontainebleau and its ancient forest, in France. His piece describing Toupie mentions not only her connection to Les Ruches[37] – a school still gliding through history with a notoriety of its own – but also to boxing, rowing and horse riding:

"Since she was very young she devoted herself to all physical exercises: horse riding, rowing, tennis and also boxing. Miss Lowther received her early fencing instruction at the age of fifteen from Macpherson's School of Fencing: then she went to France to study at Les Ruches in Fontainebleau and

---

36 The title will most easily translate as *Fencing Gentlemen of Today*. A women fencer would be "l'escrimeuse".
37 "Les Ruches": The Beehives.

gained her baccalaureate[38] at the Sorbonne in "en-sciences" in 1893."[39]

Many later writers, including Una Troubridge, have cheerfully, gloatingly even, attributed boxing as a sport which Toupie practised, although no actual evidence has ever been provided. But this snippet from de Goudourville may be a grass-roots source. Any sceptical reader of de Goudourville's volumes might well wonder whom she might actually have boxed against – another young woman or perhaps a young man?[40]

Les Ruches – "Un Pensionnat de haute couture française pour jeune filles etrangères" – had been opened in 1863 by Mlle Marie Claire Souvestre, the daughter of Emile Souvestre, a distinguished author and "homme de lettres", and her business partner Mlle Caroline Dussaut. No actual evidence that the relationship between these two women was anything other than professional has ever been uncovered: and may very well be only in the minds of the suspicious.

In 1883, when Toupie would have been aged only nine, Marie Souvestre upped and parted from Les Ruches, from France, and from Caroline Dussaut. The reasons for her move remain unclear and subject to speculation. She went to Wimbledon, to the south of London, and opened a highly successful, and not dissimilar, school for young women that was named "Allenswood". Marie Souvestre died in Wimbledon in 1905: she was taken back to and buried in Brittany. "Allenswood" closed in 1945.

---

38   There is every reason to suppose that this is so. Lt Chatenay in *Mon Journal de Quatorze–Dix Huit* also refers to Toupie as a "bachelière française."

39   Translated from the original french by the author: *Escrimeurs Contemporains* by, Henry de Goudourville (Paris 1899: Chameul editeur, 5 rue de Savoir, 5, Paris) from the Open Content Alliance E Book Collection. These two volumes seem to be his only contribution to sporting activities: no more is known about his life.

40   At this time a few women did box in public, but seemingly as an entertainment in the Music Halls of the time. Thanks to Margaret Monod and her fine collection of Victorian Music hall photographs.

Education

Caroline Dussaut continued as head teacher at Les Ruches until her death in 1887 – in mysterious circumstances, possibly connected with an overdose of the sleeping drug chloral. She is buried in the Cimetière d'Avon en Seine et Marne, near Fontainebleau. Each year, on the anniversary of her death, the girls of Les Ruches would walk to her grave in an act of remembrance and gratitude.

Marie-Françoise Bastit[41] from Rennes, a descendant of one of Marie Souvestre's three brothers, has suggested that Caroline Dussaut's sudden death may well indeed have been due to an accidental overdose of the sedative chloral; and that it would be not impossible that the unexplained overdose was the result of an established addiction, which was kept from the public.

After Mlle Caroline Dussaut's death, a Mlle Gertrude Jones-Dussaut took over as "Diréctrice". Most likely she was a young Englishwoman who had been adopted by Mlle Dussaut: the circumstances are rather obscure and any paperwork has long-since vanished, but an adoption seems to be the best explanation. Under the Napoleonic Law, an adoption imposes the hyphenated attachment of the birth surname to the new surname – hence Jones-Dussaut. Unfortunately a search for a "Gertrude Jones" who was adopted by a Frenchwoman and went to France to live has not yet come up with an absolutely firm candidate.

Les Ruches became an expensive and high-standard boarding school for young women – favoured by wealthy parents from America, Britain and the British Empire who thought that a few years in Europe would greatly benefit their daughters. These parents included the father of Daisy White,[42] a young Australian woman and a dedicated diary keeper. Her diaries have survived and contain a full description of day-to-

---

41 Thanks for Mme Bastit's encouragement and generosity.
42 Margaret Isabel White 1871–1903. Always known as Daisy.

day life at Les Ruches[43] including a mention, at one time, that Mlle Jones-Dussaut is "not at school" during a school holiday because she is "in England".

The girls at Les Ruches were given a high quality, progressive, intellectual, cultural and social education – all delivered in the French language. There was a wide curriculum: classic and cultural French literature, poetry and drawing, music and dancing, all augmented with frequent "visites" – by train from Avon-Fontainebleau station – to the lofty art galleries and imposing theatres in Paris. As well as the long galleries of the Palais du Luxembourg and the corridors of the Louvre and the Théâtre-Français. The more practical side of education was not excluded: mathematics, physics, and chemistry were also taught by visiting gentlemen "professeurs", probably students, from The Sorbonne who would always have been always ready to earn a few extra francs.

Henry de Goudourville's brief chapter on Toupie's fencing career seems to be the source for the often-repeated tag that Toupie gained a degree from the Sorbonne. There is some reason to disbelieve this. The baccalaureate is not a university degree but a school-leaving certificate of achievement, which was offered by Les Ruches – see the publicity leaflet pictured below. The Sorbonne then (as the University of Paris-Sorbonne does today) provided such an examination board for school leavers. Sadly, in translation, the word "baccalaureate" seems to have lurched rather slovenly into the academic title "Bachelor" and has been interpreted as a university degree.

The fact that pupils could be coached and then entered for the "baccalaureate examination" did not always please the journalists of the time. A sour assessment of the teaching methods at Les Ruches had been published in *Les Temps* (date

---

43 *Daisy in Exile: The Diary of an Australian Schoolgirl in France* 1887–1889 by Daisy White, introduced and annotated by Marc Serge Rivière. National Library of Australia, Canberra: 2003: see Appendix 4.

unknown), demonising the education of young women by highlighting the danger of teaching liberal ideas alongside a shocking social association with young men from the local army garrison and a menacing multitude of foreign pupils. In response, Gertrude Jones-Dussaut, in her capacity as Diréctrice, wrote: "Il y a encore des Ruches françaises à Fontainebleau, elles prospèrent et, outré l'enseignement trois langues vivantes, qui y est fortement organise, on y prepare au baccalaureate[44] avec success."[45]

It would seem in character that gaining a baccalaureate would have been Toupie's wish, and also that of her father. No other reference to Toupie's education has been uncovered. The most obvious possibility is that both she and her elder sister were taught by a governess at home until Toupie went to Les Ruches possibly to gain the baccalaureate. This would most likely be the late 1880s, some time after Mlle Souvestre had abandoned Les Ruches, France, and the death of Mlle Dussaut.

Sadly, Toupie is not mentioned in Daisy White's diary, but Mlle "Gertie" Jones is. In later years she will feature in Toupie's life as Mme Gertrude Brethous-Lafargue, the mother of her much-loved god-daughter, Fabienne Brethous Lafargue, who was born in 1901 in St Severs, Adour, near Bordeaux.[46]

Toupie's time at Les Ruches is documented only by M. de Goudourville. However, her connection with Gertrude Jones-Dussaut/Brethous-Lafargue – who can most certainly be placed at the school thanks to Daisy White – provides a firm link. There is no reason to doubt that to Les Ruches she did go, though for how long remains unknown.

---

44 Women were enabled to sit for the baccalaureate from 1880 onwards and were also admitted to universities as students. However they were not permitted to sit for and to gain a degree until much later.
45 "There are always many French young women at Les Ruches in Fontainbleau, they do well and as well as studying three modern languages, are successfully prepared for the baccalaureate." Thanks to Marie-Françoise Bastit for this information.
46 See Chapter 13.

As a school Les Ruches was closed permanently at the beginning of the Great War: the original school building, though much altered, still stands in Fontainbleau. However, in 1942, the building holding the Les Ruches archives became the victim of a German bombing raid, and nothing of Les Ruches has survived. To a great loss for study, for research, and for history.

LES RUCHES

MAISON D'ÉDUCATION
POUR LES JEUNES FILLES

FONDÉE PAR

Mlle DUSSAUT

A FONTAINEBLEAU

Le prix de la Pension est de 3,500 francs (£ 140) pour l'année scolaire et comprend tout l'enseignement :

Quatre langues vivantes :	l'Arithmétique complète,
le Français,	le Dessin ;
l'Anglais,	le Piano ;
l'Allemand,	le Chant ;
l'Italien ;	des éléments d'Harmonie,
l'Histoire générale et la Géographie ;	la danse ;
les éléments des Sciences naturelles et physiques ;	la Gymnastique ; les Travaux à l'aiguille.

Les Élèves qui font aux Ruches toute leur éducation, y suivent des cours d'enseignement secondaire faits par des Professeurs de l'Université et comprenant le Latin, le Grec, les Sciences naturelles et physiques, les Mathématiques élémentaires, et pouvant conduire aux deux Baccalauréats.

Les Ruches Publicity Prospectus.
With thanks to Marie-Françoise Bastit.

6

Sporting life: Fencing

Fencing for young ladies had become a popular form of "gentle exercise" for upper-class women in the late-Victorian era. The Prince of Wales had sent his daughters for fencing lessons (to Salle Bertrand) after he himself had taken up the sport. Naturally, these pioneers would have been swiftly followed by many daughters from wealthy and ambitious families.

"Ladies Fencing at MacPhersons, Sloane Street, 1899. Miss Toupie Lowther, on the right, is refereeing the bout".

Toupie began to fence, in her own words, between the ages of fifteen and sixteen, becoming a pupil at McPherson's Gymnasium and School of Arms[47] which was conveniently situated at 30 Sloane Street, Chelsea, near to the Lowthers' house in Pont Street. William McPherson was an ex-army instructor who was followed into the business by his three sons, William, Frederick and Henry. Indeed his daughter, not unsurprisingly, also fenced.[48] Later she became a pupil of the top French maître d'armes Camille Prévost, coming to prefer the French rather than the Italian school of fencing.

As a woman Toupie was restricted to fencing with – or against – other women: well-brought-up young ladies all – and most likely near her own age and of some social standing. Women's play was also restricted to the foil, foregoing the epée and sabre – and duelling, either for money or honourable satisfaction, would never have, in any way, been deemed socially acceptable for young women.

It seems that it was during these early days of "l'éscrime" that Toupie's prowess, performances and personality began to hit the gossip and entertainment columns of the press. In 1900 *The Sketch* described her thus: "Miss Lowther is in appearance a typical fencer, tall, graceful, alert, with keen grey/blue eyes and a magnificent complexion, the result of perfect health." She took her sport seriously, and she had firm views on dress. She abandoned the regular divided fencing skirt and championed white or black knickerbockers beneath the fencer's padded jacket (plastron), maintaining: "It is impossible to fence in a skirt."[49]

She may well have been confident of approval. The graceful (but often acidic) Society columnist Lady Violet

---

47 Salle d'Armes.
48 See also Appendix 5 and *The Wheelwoman* (inc. the *Sportswoman* and *The Woman Cyclist* (London) 14th May 1898.
49 *Evening Telegraph* 6th May 1898: The Newspaper Archive. The divided fencing skirt worn by women is reminiscent of the old serge gymslip. It was heavily pleated and usually of a dark colour, falling discreetly to about knee height.

Greville, writing in her gubernatorial column "Place aux Dames" with no hint of disapproval, describes Toupie as "attired in the neatest of white coats and knickerbockers" and adding: "She showed surprising skill and agility."[50]

With many thanks to Malcolm Fare, National Fencing Museum.

On tour nationwide giving fencing demonstrations, often for charity, her appearances could pull in the crowds and always seem to have delighted the press. "Miss Toupie Lowther – of fencing renown – is to come down from London… she showed surprising skill and ability…" "Miss Toupie Lowther has also promised to give an exhibition of Fencing [at the Royalty Theatre]. Tickets one guinea and half a guinea from the box-office." Local newspapers all cheerfully reported her appearances.[51]

Even that most senior weekly women's top drawer magazine *The Lady* joined in. In November 1899 "The Lady Debating Society" ran a feature heavily headlined "SHOULD WOMEN FENCE" – offering vigorously approving contributions from Miss Toupie Lowther, Lady Colin Campbell, Miss Janette Steer and Mlle Hélène Bertrand.[52]

Toupie writes:

"The question has often been put to me "What is the use of women learning to fence?" It teaches them to gain command over their limbs, and tends a great deal

---

50 *The Graphic*, 24th December 1898.
51 British Newspaper Archive online, inter alia the *Morning Post* London, the *Dundee Courier*, the *Yorkshire Evening Post*, the *Blackburn Standard*.
52 A daughter of M. Baptiste Bertrand who owned a Salle d' Armes in Regent Street, London.

to correct that faulty peculiarity for which English women are noted – stiffness! Apart from according physical exercise, it taxes the brain to no small degree. You not only have to prepare and carry out your attack with incredible swiftness, but must almost simultaneously be on your guard..."[53]

One of Toupie's most widely acclaimed victories came on 30th April 1898, when she competed at a widely publicised competition and display held at The Military Gymnasium of the Army Camp in Aldershot. The display was organised by Egerton Castle,[54] the celebrated swordsman, and Sir Frederick Pollock, Bart, the then president of the Oxford University Fencing Club. Both men were well known and popular gentleman fencers.

This was a prestigious exhibition. The publicity announced that "the display has been arranged mainly for the sake of encouraging fencing among women". There was general fencing, prizes for winners and for style, demonstrations and musical interludes.

A special train was chartered to run from London to Aldershot to bring spectators. It was the first event of its kind ever held in England. There were over 500 people present, and enthusiastic reports appeared widely in the press.

The afternoon proved a notable success. Opposing both other women fencers as well as the army sergeant instructor, Toupie acquitted herself well. She staggered the onlookers by vanquishing her lady opponents and, to everyone's amazement – and to the overwhelming delight of the audience and press – by defeating the sergeant instructor himself.

---

53   *The Lady*, 30th November 1899 headed "Miss Toupie Lowther dwells on fencing's expediency". *The Lady* has been in continuous publication since 1885.
54   Egerton Castle, 1858– 920. His book *Schools and Masters of Fencing From the Middle Ages to the Eighteenth Century.* pub. 1884 is available online.

Clearly the occasion was a momentous one. Even the *New York Times* reported the event on 15 May 1898 in its column "The Past Week in Society".⁵⁵

Toupie was later interviewed by a reporter from the *Evening Telegraph*, who gratifyingly headlined her as "THE WORLD'S CHAMPION LADY FOIL FENCER" and then as "THE BEST LADY FENCER WITH THE FOILS IN THE WORLD". The reporter describes her as tall, strong, and handsome with a fine healthy complexion, clear eyes and black hair. The interviewer goes on to extract from her that she considers herself still learning, that she is in fact "studying in Paris with Desmedt, the Belgian champion, and has plans to fence in Brussels later in the year". She adds that she is also in Paris to learn singing, and has always "gone in for" riding, rowing, swimming and lawn tennis.

However, she went on in the interview to add, rather unfortuitously, that "the English do not really know how to fence". With the defeat of the sergeant instructor probably still stinging in some quarters, there followed an angry exchange of letters in the newspapers, and a delicately poised suggestion that "Captain Alfred Hutton the well known and respected and celebrated swordsman and a renowned instructor could teach even so redoubtable a person as Miss Lowther a few points in either the Italian or French styles."⁵⁶

Her father came to her rescue and, on her behalf, challenged Captain Hutton, and any other English gentleman, to a fencing contest, the loser to pay £50 to the Prince of Wales Hospital Fund.

Captain Hutton, after some thought, responded manfully that this suggestion was an "impertinence" and that a "meeting" for a wager might disqualify both himself and

---

55 inter alia: The Newspaper Archive, *The Times* online and a multitude of other archived newspapers.
56 Actual author unnamed.

Miss Lowther as amateurs. At the time he was over sixty years old and Toupie's father was confined to his bath chair. Honour was seen to be still in place on all sides, however. (This episode is fully described in *A Proper Spectacle: Women Olympians 1900–1936*.)[57]

In 1902, Toupie opposed (and worsted) the famous lady French champion, Mme Gabrièle. The salon was crowded and Toupie seems to have acquitted herself, as usual, with elegance and pride. Clearly it was regarded as highly essential that the event be recorded for posterity, if not by photograph then by a skilled hand![58]

Toupie's fame was also known across the pond in NewYork: "Some of the woman fencers in this country are remarkably expert in execution of the various thrusts, parries and feints, and Miss Toupie Lowther, the well-known champion of the English women's fencing world, is more than a match for many a man that considers himself a capable performer. Miss Toupie Lowther, the Englishwoman fencer, is enthusiastically lauded in some of the Paris papers for her recent bout of arms at the Civil Engineers Hall in the Rue Blanche… Miss Lowther tried the foils with Maître, or Prof Yvon, and was applauded as she stepped forth in her white plastron, and knickers [sic], her black silk stockings and patent leather shoes. She is said to have held her own remarkably well against the stern male professional, and she received as a trophy a "foil of honor" ornamented with white ribbons and lilac…"[59]

---

57 By Stephanie Daniels and Anita Tedder (ZeNaNA Press, 2000). In fact, the dice were loaded against Captain Hutton. As a gentleman he could not, in any way, accept a challenge from either a young woman or a man in a wheelchair with no use of his legs. Had he done so, most likely his reputation as a gentleman would have been shredded.
58 See book cover.
59 Spalding's Athletic Library, *The Art of Fencing* by Regis and Louis Senac, New York professional Champions of America. Published by the American Sports Publishing Company, 15 Warren Street, New York 1904; the Newspaper Archive.

"This week saw a very remarkable entertainment in London. It was a fencing bout at the Ladies' Army and Navy Club... with Miss Toupie Lowther, the baronne [Olga] de Meyer and the princesse de Polignac [Winnaretta Singer][60] who appears not infrequently in Paris in visits to Natalie Barney... Miss Lowther also fenced with some of the men victors in several of the contests.[12] However, a well-publicised mixed bout between Toupie and a Captain Senat[61] – the director de la section d'escrime of the famous Joinville school – did not impress the reporter. He (presumably "he") writes: "It was unfortunate that Miss Lowther should have been matched against him rather than one of her own sex. Captain Senac confined himself to a courteous defensive, but Miss Lowther had no opportunity of showing her undoubted capabilities." The reporter adds, "mixed fencing is nearly always unsatisfactory and this event was no exception to the rule".

The *Black & White* magazine of 27th February 1904 includes a drawing of Olga de Meyer with Toupie and Mrs Newton Robinson wife of Charles Newton Robinson, founder of The Epée Club in 1900 at the second Assault des Armes held at The Empress Rooms, The Royal Palace Hotel Kensington[62] on the evening of 20th February.

After 1904, now coming up to thirty years of age, Toupie gradually started to abandon competitive fencing – although

---

60 Thanks to "The Tennis Ware-house" webpages.
61 Most likely Louis Senac, a well know fencer of the time. See L'Ecole Militaire de Joinville en France 1852-1939.
62 Sadly demolished in the 1960s and replaced by The Royal Garden Hotel.

she avidly maintained her interest in the sport by becoming chairman of the ladies' Cercle d'Escrime. In December 1909 she did turn out for Salle Mimiague at a team competition for the first Ladies' Inter-salle Challenge Cup – alongside Mrs Edwards (Capt.) and Olga de Meyer – losing, however, to the team from Salle Bertrand. This could well have been the final tournament of Toupie's actual competitive fencing career – other references refer to exhibitions only.

By 1911 Toupie was approaching her later thirties. But the press still continued to notice: *The Times* reported that she had "put in" an appearance in the audience at an Assault des Armes at the Actors Sword Club and Actresses Foil Club at Professor Gravé's School of Arms. A rapier and dagger display and contests with foil, epée and sabre – prizes a pair of epées and a pair of foils – were won by Miss Gracie Leigh.[63]

In 1913, at the sixtieth Anniversary of Salle Bertrand, although no longer quite the young and adorable athlete that she had been ten years previously, Toupie was in a celebrated audience of well-known fencers and maîtres d'armes in the Victoria Hall of the Hotel Cecil.[64] The occasion was a fabulous afternoon and evening display of arms and exhibition foil play, including an appearance by Miss Gladys Daniell, the then women's foil champion. An impressive list of leading English and Belgian fencing celebrities also attended.[65]

Some reporters were still keen to write about her even a good few years later. In 1926, an anonymous gossip columnist reported that Miss Toupie Lowther "has recently been elected (unanimously) a member of the 'Academie d'Armes' in France… the only woman ever admitted to this historic body since its foundation." At the time, qualification for the award of this honour would have demanded a known status as maître d'armes: this requirement was not abandoned until 2013 and

---

63 *The Times*, 17th June 1911.
64 A grand hotel said to have had at least 800 rooms. Demolished 1930.
65 *The Times*, 23rd April 1913.

Sporting Life: Fencing

this triumphant reporting should be read with some caution. Indeed, the archivist at the Academie d'Armes has, sadly, been unable to find any indication that this happy award event ever happened.[66]

In 1938, now in her mid-sixties and many years away from the bouts, exhibitions and competitive matches, it is a measure of the still-remaining respect for her swordsmanship that *The Times* asked Toupie to write the obituary for Camille Prévost, the late honorary President of the Académie d'Armes de Paris. She writes, inter alia, "with the passing of Camille Prévost the entire world have [sic] lost one of the greatest fencers of all time".[67]

Looking back to the first modern Olympic Games of 1896, the Fencing programme consisted of men's foil and sabre events, with the epée making its debut at the Paris Games of 1900.

At the time, women's competitive fencing was still strictly limited to the use of the lightest weapon – the foil. A women's foil event was first featured at the Paris Olympic Games of 1924. Very much more recently the epée and the sabre have been introduced: an epée competition for women featured in the 1996 Games, and a sabre competition in Athens in 2004.

It is a measure of Toupie's standing in the history of women's fencing that in *A Proper Spectacle: Women Olympians 1900–1936*[68] she receives more than just a passing glance. Chapter 4, "One Step Forward Two Steps Back" has a fine tribute to her, despite the fact that Toupie did not fence at any Olympic Games. That she is included in *A Proper Spectacle* indicates the quality of a reputation that has travelled down the years.

A "Toupie Lowther Cup" was initiated by the Ladies' Amateur Fencing Union as a competition for unclassified

---

66 *The Sunday Times*, 25th April 1926. Correspondence from *The Academie d'Armes*, France.
67 *The Times*, 11th August 1938.
68 See also http://www.olympicwomen.co.uk. Thanks to Malcolm Fare, National Fencing Museum.

women fencers. The competition was held in October every year until 1988, after which it was discontinued: sadly the whereabouts of the cup itself are not known.

Toupie in full kit, a photo widely known and often reproduced from, inter alia, the Sketch, *1st June 1898. The photograph seems to be from an original photo by W. and D. Downey, Ebury Street. Most likely she has been photographed as a younger woman who is still living at home with her family. She may be in fencing knickerbockers but her hair is still uncropped.*

Toupie Lowther's Bookplate. The motto reads Vouloir est Pouvoir – To Desire is To Achieve. Note the crossed foils. With thanks to Tony Wolf.

7

SPORTING LIFE:
TENNIS AND OTHER SPORTS

By 1900 lawn tennis, for both men and women, had become a sport both to play and to watch. The game offered a wide variety of competitive play to onlookers: men's, women's, and even mixed matches played on grass in the sunshine or on wood inside a covered hall. The game was overwhelmingly popular: home and international tournaments were flourishing and a circuit of championships had been instituted in Great Britain – at Edgebaston, Beckenham, Manchester, Leicester and Wimbledon to name but a few – and in various European countries and the USA. Germany and France and Great Britain topped the popularity poll of the European countries.

Toupie regularly travelled to and played competitively in the major tournaments, as did the other mighty women tennis names of the time: Blanche Hillyard, Charlotte Sterry, Dorothea Douglass (later Mrs Lambert Chambers), May Sutton, Lottie Dod, Elsie Lane, Charlotte Cooper, and many others whose names may or may not have survived into the glow of sporting history. A dedicated driver of fast cars, Toupie invariably drove herself to, from, and across Europe: not necessarily as a permanently prestigious winner who acquired many victories, but as one who ought to. Her fans were often disappointed, but were always forgiving.

Weekly and monthly magazines, always hungry for news of the goings on of celebrities from all classes, then as now, widely followed both competitive and demonstration matches and sporting activities. Some tournaments naturally would attract a higher status than others. The German tennis competition, the Championship of the Germans was always held at Hamburg – but was however only open to German and Austrian players. The later German Championship and the "German Ladies Championship" – hosted by the Homburg Lawn Tennis Club from 1896 to 1901, – were open to all nationalities.

Bad Homburg Spa was not only an international and highly popular hot spring resort, offering both drinking and bathing cures at the local mineral and saltwater springs, but also hosted the summer residence of the German royal family. Their fine summer palace directly faced the tight green spread of neatly trimmed tennis courts, and members of the royal family were often to be spotted practising their strokes at the royal nets.

However it was not to last. After 1901 Bad Homburg was abandoned and the German Championships reverted to the larger town, no doubt to much disappointment from both players and onlookers (albeit that the hotels, the courts, and the general transport links may well have been more accessible). And this is where, except during the two world wars, it has stayed.

Not all the details of Toupie's matches have survived, but some have passed into history. What comes across from the accounts is a fine and personally-popular player, who could wring support and enthusiasm from the onlookers… but who would then dramatically and despairingly mislay her skill and finish on the losing side of the match. In 1898, she played Elsie Lane: a "brilliant, albeit erratic, Toupée [sic] Lowther who had abandoned her usual play in favour of an uninspired game from base line" lost in two straight sets, 7–5, 7–5. In 1899 she lost in an early round to Charlotte Sterry: after winning the first set she managed to lose six games in a row, finally losing in the third set. But in 1901 Toupie did win the Ladies' Championship at Homburg, defeating Gladys Duddell 6–0, 6–0. The reward, a silver dish.

In 1906, at the German Tournament in Baden-Baden, she made it through to the women's singles final but was beaten by Dorothea Douglass 6–4, 6–4. A fellow member of the Hillyard circle and a fixture on the Hillyard's visiting list at their country home, The Elms, in the village of Thorpe Satchville, Leicestershire, the two would have been well known to each other. But Dorothea Douglass had the staying power. She became a seven-time winner of the Women's Championship at Wimbledon: in 1911 she won the women's final 6–0, 6–0, a feat only repeated by Steffi Graff at the French Open Championships in 1988.[69]

Toupie played regularly – and usually gallantly – at Wimbledon (the courts and club house were then in Worple Road) for the All England Women's Championships, going down early on in the tournament to that terrifyingly formidable player Blanche Hillyard in 1902. In 1903 she got as far as the singles semi-final before losing, this time to Dorothea Douglass, 6–4, 6–2.

In 1906 Toupie again reached the women's singles semi-final, but lost this time to Charlotte Sterry, 4–6, 8–6, 6–4.

Victory, however, did not always elude: gratifyingly Toupie managed to gain the Women's Singles British Covered

---

69 *Tennis, a Cultural History* by Heiner Gillmeister (Leicester University Press, 1997). The Tennis Forum, The Early Ladies' Championships of Germany: Talk Tennis 2010.

Well-known image probably from The Bystander, 19th June 1907: "Lawn Tennis at Beckenham – Studies in expression and attitude".

Championships in 1900 and then again in 1902 and 1903. (She went down to Blanche Hillyard in 1901.)[70]

Although magnificent international wins avoided her game, and she did not ever achieve that tip-top Wimbledon championship trophy, the mighty Silver Dish of the All England Tennis Women's Championships, the mettle of her opponents, and the interest of the tennis journalists, would indicate an individual quality in Toupie's play. Her on-court personality seems to have been able to draw a warmly enthusiastic audience in spite of her losses, and she is described with great affection by the writers of the time. Today she would most likely be regarded as a "character player", who frequently – though not always – would groaningly disappoint her audience when her "temperament" ruthlessly stepped in and hindered her play.

The Badminton Magazine[71] in a series called "Masters of their Arts" published a piece "Lawn Tennis" by Toupie Lowther in April 1903. The piece – both gently advisory and name-droppingly reminiscent – is written in her light but delicate prose: "I now come to the stroke which is perhaps the most difficult, I mean the overhead smash. Among the few whom

---

70 http://www.enotes.com/topic/British_Covered_Court_Championships.

71 *The Badminton Magazine* was very popular and appeared in the shops from 1885 to at least 1923. No manner of sport is said to have escaped its pages.

nature has endowed with the capability of nearly always bringing off this stroke are G.W. Hillyard, H.S. Mahoney and the two Dohertys. H.L. Doherty's smash is particularly characterised by the admirable way in which it is placed: Hillyard's by its great severity. Both have the same object, which is that their smash should be unreturnable: both attain it by different methods."[72]

The Doherty brothers, Reginald and Hugh Laurence,[73] also asked Toupie if she would write a chapter for their book *Lawn Tennis*. Her chapter is headed "Ladies' Play" and starts off with what seems to be a jarring condemnation, describing the inferiority of women's tennis. Looking more closely, however, her target is not the woman player per se – but her mandatory long-skirted dress:

"It is curious to note what a marked inferiority there is in the ladies' game as compared to the men's' if one takes the best representatives of both sexes... I think it is a pity a regulation costume keeping with the game is not enforced. A lady's modesty does not prevent her from doing gymnastics... dressed in garments befitting the occasion: and yet she will appear on a tennis court in skirts often so long that she is in danger of falling over them and injuring herself, not to speak of losing the stroke, game or match... Surely there is a just medium all things and there is no reason why they should not wear short skirts, well above the ankles."[74]

In 1924 George Hillyard, the mighty All England Tennis Club Secretary for many years and husband of Blanche Hillyard, wrote of Toupie Lowther, both despairingly and lovingly at the same time:

---

72 *The Badminton Magazine*, Masters Of Their Arts No. XV1 – Lawn Tennis.
73 The Doherty brothers were both English born players.
74 Quoted in *Playing the Game: Sport and the Physical Emancipation of English Women 1870–1914*, by Kathleen E. McCrone (University Press of Kentucky, 1988).

"Here is the extraordinary case of a player whose potentialities were greater than any other English lady who ever walked onto a court, but who, unfortunately was saddled with a temperament which was so hopelessly unsuitable to lawn tennis that it reduced her play… not one, but at least two classes below what her form should have been… It is no flight of imagination to say that had Miss Lowther been blessed with the temperament of a Mrs Sterry or a Mrs Lambert Chambers [Dorothea Douglass], she might have been as fine a player as Mlle Lenglen herself."

Yet following this cry of both admiration and despair, he includes "a characteristic contribution from that fine player and delightful personality, Miss Toupie Lowther… she calls it 'An Episode at Homburg'… to which my appreciation would be superfluous." No other contribution from any of the many sporting personalities who feature in the book are awarded this privilege. The "contribution", written in Toupie's characteristic flowing and decorative language, is a description of the very first match ever played between herself and Blanche Hillyard. Toupie writes:

"The shock to my nervous system was very severe when told I had to play Mrs. Hillyard – Mrs. Hillyard, the innumerable times Champion! So much so, that when I walked into the court, and began the match, the balls seemed to have shrunk to the size of marbles, the nets to have stretched in height like Alice in Wonderland… imbued with a demon-like ability [she] placed that wretched little ball wherever she liked and wherever I was not… I swore to myself (it seemed that swearing was the only faculty left to me) that never would I play a tournament again…"

During the match Toupie lost the first set 1–6. However she goes on to narrate that, when "crossing over", Mrs Hillyard applied the spine-stiffening stick: "Why on earth don't you try? It is perfectly sickening playing someone who doesn't try. Don't be such a d---- fool! Stick to it and you will win."

Toupie continues: "the effect of this encouragement by a total stranger and still more the drastic and peculiar method of giving it was magical... my nervousness left me entirely and I won the match!"[75]

Photo of Toupie, from George Hillyard. The Man Who Moved Wimbledon, *by Bruce Tarrant (Matador, 2013). With many thanks.*

Other Sports

Motor Cars

Many references to Toupie indicate her love for fast cars. Dorothea Lambert Chambers quotes what was clearly a not infrequent experience.

"... the touring abroad is both an education and a delight. Monte Carlo, Nice, Cannes, Homburg, Baden-Baden and Dinard, all bring the pleasantest reminiscences. Many of us have travelled about together, which is the jolliest way of doing the tournaments. I remember one most enjoyable

---

75 *Forty Years of First Class Lawn Tennis*, G. W. Hillyard (William & Norgate Ltd, 1924).

trip, when Miss Lowther motored the Hillyards and myself through Germany – an ideal way of doing tournaments!"[76]

In 1906 Toupie was driving a forty-horse power Mercedes. In 1917, on her journey to France, a six-cylinder Wolseley. In 1922 in Brighton with Una Troubridge and Radclyffe Hall she buys an "Overland Tourer"[77] and teaches them to drive it! She was certainly caught speeding at least once.

"Miss Lowther, 13 Upper Brook street, London W, was a victim to the [speed] trap between Spittlegate and Great Ponton on 7th October… the police officers timed her to travel the 2½ miles in 4½ minutes – at a speed of 33½ miles per hour. Defendant's chauffeur represented Miss Lowther and said he had come to plead guilty. Fined £4 and costs."[78]

Boxing and Jujitsu

Toupie is often described as having tried her hand at the very physical arts of both boxing and jujitsu. Neither is totally unbelievable, if and when confined to being practised in a gym. But it would seem very unlikely that "Miss Toupie Lowther", as a young woman, in public, ever boxed against an opponent, which is what is implied. Yet many later writers, including Una Troubridge, have cheerfully, gloatingly even, attributed boxing as a sport which Toupie practised, although no actual evidence has ever been forthcoming. At the time, public boxing for women was restricted to common fairground travelling circus entertainment and was regarded as bordering on the edge of prostitution. Her father would never have allowed himself to permit such a display, and that top-class magazine beloved of the nobility, *The Lady,* would not have even contemplated inviting

---

76 *Lawn Tennis for Ladies*, by Dorothea Chambers (Methuen & Co., 1910); now available from Dodo Press.
77 A handsome four-cylinder soft convertible classic car now highly sought after.
78 "Kesteven Motor Traps", 24th October 1908. A clip from a newspaper, original unknown.

the perpetrator of such a scandalous event to write for its pages.

However, Toupie was never one to take heed in front of opposition. As a young and athletic woman it is by no means impossible that she did "put on the gloves", but very likely for exercising the strength of her arms, as well as the agility of her legs and the stamina of her back. Moreover, it could be quite likely that she tried her hand at jujitsu, or possibly even "Bartitsu" – known as the "Gentlemanly Art of Self-Defence" – a sport that was highly popular at the turn of the century and by no means forbidden to women.[79]

Horse Riding

It would be impossible to imagine that Toupie did not ride. That she could get up on a horse, in full kit, and gallop into and back from any nearby hills, inspires no disbelief. No details or other references seem to have survived other than the photograph below. Her seat is firm, her riding kit impeccable, the horse docile and seemingly under control. Clearly, she is no stranger to the sport.

Toupie and horse. With thanks to Paul Handford.

---
79 See Appendix 5.

This magnificent photo was most likely taken in France during the Hackett Lowther Ambulance Unit's sojourn there during the Great War or possibly after the Armistice, in 1918/19.

Golf

No particular newspaper reference to Toupie as a golf player has yet been discovered, but there is every reason to suppose that this sport did not pass her by. In 1932, when she was probably living – or intending to live – in West Sussex, she presented a trophy, "The Lowther Challenge Cup", to The West Sussex Golf Club, near Pulborough, to be awarded to women players. The competition is still played today as an open thirty-six-hole scratch event for ladies, and the handsome silver bowl is always on display. The first winner was Joyce Wethered, who retains a reputation as the greatest lady golfer this country has even produced.[80] The inscription reads:

LOWTHER CHAMPIONSHIP BOWL
WEST SUSSEX GOLF CLUB CHAMPIONSHIP
PRESENTED BY T. LOWTHER

---

80   Thanks to Andy Stubbs, Secretary, West Sussex Golf Club.

8

The Batten Diaries

The most frequently quoted – and thus the most widely known references to Toupie – are her walk-on appearances, both sporadically and in clusters, in the diaries of first Mabel Batten, from 1910 onwards, and then of Una Troubridge from 1919.

Mabel, Mrs George Batten, known as "Ladye" (1856–1916) was acquainted with Toupie Lowther – and possibly Toupie's brother Claude – from at least 1906 and possibly even before. Married to George Batten in 1874 and presenting him with a daughter, Cara, hers was a rich, cultured, and leisured life.

She had a fine mezzo-soprano voice and, like many sociable, well-poised and positioned women, was known as an accomplished singer, pianist, and guitar player. And as a well-regarded composer of drawing-room songs. One of her best-known compositions was a setting of "The Queen's Last Ride" – a poem by Ella Wheeler

Portrait of Mabel as a young woman. With thanks to Cara Lancaster.

Wilcox written for Queen Victoria's funeral – which was widely praised.

The British Library holds thirteen of Mabel Batten's songs in manuscript – rather more indeed than the solitary four of Toupie's music. With music in common it would seem likely that Toupie and Mrs Batten may well have become known to each other before they are first recorded as being in the same place at the same time. The "music" thread appears often in Toupie's life.

The terrace at the Savoy Hotel. With grateful thanks to Beate Datzkow from the Bad Homburg Tourist office.

As a connoisseuse of travel, art, and good living, always superbly dressed and surrounded by an amusing and gifted circle of friends and admirers, on 9th August 1906 Mabel Batten arrived at Homburg with her husband George.

No doubt they were there to take excellent advantage of the famed hot-mineral springs, long celebrated for their healing and health-enhancing powers. They stayed at The Savoy Hotel in Kisseleffstrasse – where else – and happily entertained their friends on the Savoy's terrace.

Toupie and her father were also staying in Homburg, having arrived on 31st July. They stayed in private accommodation at the Haus Braun, Ferdinandstrasse 24. The local records indicate that they had visited Homburg together a few years before. In very poor health now, with no use in his legs and confined to his bath chair, it would seem very likely that Francis Lowther had returned to Bad Homburg for another summer of long-soaking visits to the Homburg Spa.

Postcard of The Savoy Hotel, Homburg in 1906. With grateful thanks to Beate Datzkow from the Bad Homburg Tourist Office, 2013. The Savoy Hotel was demolished in the 1970s.

Bad Homburg was, and still is, well known as a fine spa town; its famous, gushing, healing springs of natural water attracting visitors from all across Europe. By 1906 the prestigious international tennis tournaments, well known to Toupie, had moved away from Homburg to the rather bigger, but not necessarily as pleasantly situated, town of Hamburg. But Homburg was still the summer home of the German royal family, the palace looking out onto their own courts.

Another visitor to the spa town that summer was the poet Marguerite Radclyffe Hall. She came to Homburg a day or so after the Lowthers, on 2nd August 1906, and also stayed in Ferdinandstrasse in private accommodation. It would seem possible that this may have been when Marguerite (soon to be renamed John) Radclyffe Hall first became acquainted with Mabel Batten and her daughter Cara – or even with Toupie. Whenever the Mabel/Marguerite friendship came to blossom into a five-year love affair, Toupie remained as a friend to both: and often appears in Mabel's diaries as a side player, known to both partners, in their busy cultural and social life. Mabel's diaries are by no means widely descriptive of time and events; they are more a scribbling down of the solitary name of whom she had lunch with, and where, or had visited on a nice day out.

Back in gas-lit and horse-drawn London between 1910 and 1915, lunches and theatre visits with friends are recorded – some greater, some lesser. Toupie visits Mabel and John at home; they lunch at The Grill in Hyde Park. A threesome of Mabel, Mabel's daughter Cara and Toupie go to see *Trelawney of the "Wells* – a comic play by Arthur Wing Pinero, first shown in 1898 – and in 1910 Mabel, Cara and John, after dinner, go to the Palace Theatre to see the famous Russian ballerina Anna Pavlova on stage. In 1911 there are no mentions of Toupie – possibly she was on one her French sojourns.

Mabel's social diary indicates that the threesome of herself, John, and Toupie meet up again early in 1912 in London – lunch, again at The Grill Room in Hyde Park, and in 1914 Mabel, John and Toupie, along with "Bobby" Clarke, go to the opera for a performance of *Madam Butterfly*: two weeks later Bobby and Toupie have a box to see the last night of the Russian opera *Coq d'Or* and later Gluck's opera *Echo and Narcisse*. Mabel and John go with them.

Robert Coningsby Clarke – Bobby Clarke – was a successful musician and composer. He set to music John's most famous poem, *The Blind Ploughman*, which became a very popular song. Today it would probably be counted as a serious bestseller. And can still be heard, on YouTube, in several versions – close to a hundred years after its composition. Clark married John's cousin (and possibly one-time lover), Dolly Diehl, in 1909.

On Saturday, 21st June 1913, Toupie, Mabel and John paid a Sussex visit to Toupie's brother Claude William Henry Lowther at his moated and stonily-turreted home in Sussex, Herstmonceux Castle. They stayed for the weekend – Mabel occupying the supposedly haunted "Drummer's room" (her night seems to have been undisturbed). On the Sunday they met "Kenny Cunningham",[81] and on the Monday they walked with Claude to see a cottage in the grounds that he had had built for his and Toupie's mother,

---

81   Kenneth Cunningham features in Claude Lowther's will as an equal beneficiary with Claude Michael John Barrington. Nothing more is known about him.

Louise. After luncheon, Toupie with them, they drove back to London.

Later in the year in September, Toupie took Mabel and John to the Hillyards' substantial country home for a short holiday[82] "The Elms": a large house near the village of Thorpe Satchville in Leicestershire. There were many guest bedrooms, and two tennis courts, a nine-hole golf course, stables and kennels. They watched Toupie play tennis with George Hillyard and G. C. Ball-Greene – an Irish player who "considered Miss Lowther to be the finest stroke player of any lady". John, Toupie and the others went riding: Mabel "sang a lot". On the 27th Mabel was persuaded to get into the saddle herself, and everyone played "absurd poker" in the evening. However, during the night, to add to the excitement, there was a burglar scare: "Awake nearly all night" Mabel records. On the 28th, no doubt feeling exhausted, the three visitors went back to London.

No one could ever describe Mabel Batten as a woman who would actively seek to engage in all-day sporting activities – tennis, golf, riding, hunting with beagles are all high-energy recreations that were always on tap at Thorpe Satchville. Yet she stayed for a week, she sang for the company and, although clearly rattled by the suspect intruder, had no impatient words about her stay to record in her diary. Mabel and John clearly felt at ease with Toupie and she with them. Indeed, by 1913 they could all three be well described as old friends.

Both Toupie and Mabel were accomplished musicians and composers. Six of Mabel Batten's compositions are housed at the British Library in a bound volume.

Mabel was a woman with what would now be known as "a high boredom threshold", and had reached a stage in her life when she demanded friends who were unusual, interesting, entertaining, and never boring. Toupie, without doubt, could clearly satisfy all of these qualities. Mabel's invented term

---

82 See Appendix 6.

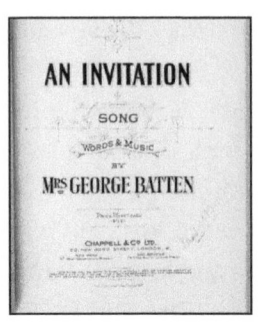

Song and accompaniment "An Invitation", held by the British Library in a bound edition of many compositions.

for dull and uninteresting people was "porkish" – and "porkish" Toupie Lowther very certainly was not.

There is every reason to suppose that Mabel Batten – and John Radclyffe Hall – liked and appreciated her company. The Toupie Lowther who appears in Mabel Batten's diaries is social, generous, and cultured: no complaints about her, from either the diarist or her partner, are recorded.

In August 1914 the war that was meant to end all wars started, and in August 1915, John Radclyffe Hall and Una Troubridge met each other, explosively, and to the detriment of her years with Mabel. "[Mabel's] friends including Adela,[83] Winnaretta[84] and Toupie, remained faithful, trying to support the older friend and understand the newer one".[85]

After the separation Mabel began an emotional and physical decline into what would lead to terminal ill health. After her miserable death on 25th May 1916, Una Troubridge and John Radclyffe Hall walked away hand-in-hand and set up house(s) together.

In echoes of earlier times, Toupie seems to have remained as a friend to both. And after her wartime adventures with the French army, she would be launched into her second round of walk-on stage appearances – but this time into the acidic pages of Una Troubridge's diaries.

---

83   Adela Maddison (1862–1929), a prolific and highly regarded composer of instrumental and orchestral music and opera, ballet and songs. It would seem, however, that much of her music has not survived.
84   Née Singer (1865–1943), the wealthy American married to the Prince de Polignac. She was a gifted musician (see also Appendix 9).
85   Aptly quoted by Sally Cline in *Radclyffe Hall, A Woman called John* (Faber & Faber, 1997).

It cannot go without mention that Toupie may very well – in fact, one would suggest almost certainly – have been acquainted with Mabel Batten well before the 1906 trip to Homburg. The connection is not only social but musical: a mutual social or professional acquaintance with the many women composers of the time. Possibly she was also known to Marguerite Radcliffe Hall, which would explain the choice of lodgings in the same Strasse at the same time.

Mabel Batten at "The White Cottage".
Photograph reproduced with kind permission from
Cara Lancaster.

9

THE HACKETT LOWTHER AMBULANCE UNIT

In 1914, when the mighty German army first flowed westward into Belgium and then eastward towards Russia, Toupie Lowther was forty years old. The attention of the newspaper reporters, who had once been avid for her appearances and comments, had, not unreasonably, drifted away. Her whereabouts during the first years of the war remain unknown and other than a brief and not particularly reliable reference to her "driving an ambulance in France" from a small newspaper cutting , any admiring journalistic references to her activities are not to be found. Post-war energetic tales describing her whereabouts between 1914 and 1917 seem not to have been either published nor ever recorded.

Yet it is almost unbelievable that she would not have embraced the national desire to participate in the war effort. A wild guess, and with no actual evidence of any sort, might be flagged up. By 1914 she was coming up to middle-age, unmarried, and of very comfortable and fully-independent means. Tall and strong, she was fluent in both French and German, and had regularly hobnobbed with nobility across the tennis courts of pre-war Germany. With a brother a Member of Parliament, who in September 1914 was busy putting together his "Southdown Battalion" of the Royal Sussex Regiment, and their cousin, Hugh, Lord Lonsdale, forming the 11th Battalion of the Border Regiment[86] at the same time, one can only conclude that if neither the British nor the French intelligence services managed to scoop her up for some kind of silent work abroad – they most surely let slip a platinum opportunity.

Unfortunately, in reply to a mildly-worded letter of enquiry, the British SIS gently remarked: "As you may know, it is the longstanding policy of the Secret Intelligence Service to neither confirm nor deny whether records of any individuals are held."

However one regards the incoming tide of war towards Belgium and France, not to mention Serbia, Roumania, Turkey and Palestine etc. towards even the shores of distant Africa both west and east, Toupie Lowther was not a woman who would allow the almost worldwide activity generated by the conflict to pass her by. Nursing was not really her style. But another overwhelmingly practical opportunity, not forbidden to women, was readily available: she could drive. And drive with vigour any heavy, speedy, chassis sprung and rubber tyred, long bonneted, noisy and seriously mighty motor car.

The participation of women volunteers in WWI has gradually become a rich source of historical research. However Toupie would never have been at her best serving in a lesser capacity under the strictures of independent ambulance organisation, even had she managed to slide past any age limit.[87] So in 1917, three years into the war, she sought to find for herself an independent and more dominant role: to

---
86 Known as "The Lonsdales".
87 The First Aid Nursing Yeomanry, known as the FANY, was a fine supplier of ambulance drivers in France and Belgium. However the organisation imposed an age limit of twenty for drivers.

organise, to put together, to lead and to direct her own All Women Ambulance Unit. A unit, moreover, which would have no age limit, and would gracefully offer its services not to the stubbornly anti-women's-involvement British Army, but to the mighty Army of the French: with a view to operating as close up to and as near to the action as it was possible for any woman to be.

The time that Toupie launched her Ambulance and Canteen Unit, mid-1917, is so accurately fortuitous that it is hard to believe that her timing was not deliberately planned. The withdrawal of Russia from the war following the 1917 Revolution followed by the fully anticipated subsequent peace treaty of Brest-Litovsk early in the following year,[88] would inevitably free up a multitude of German forces from the Eastern Front and it was inevitable that a new German advance would be launched westward in some hurry. Before the full might of the American armies could arrive in Europe.

The Hackett Lowther Canteen and Motor Ambulance Unit began to be put together in later 1917, and some good publicity projected her back into the public gaze. References and memories of her past sporting achievements attracted the hungry attention of reporters and soon there was no shortage of volunteers. Women who could afford to bring their own vehicle with them were very welcome and those who could not would have one provided. There was no age barrier.

And the Hackett Lowther Unit would be different. The All Women Ambulance Unit would serve, if necessary under fire, on the Western Allied front line. This was unheard of for women drivers, who hitherto had always been placed fairly well back from the front and in no kind of danger from enemy action. Toupie knew – or possibly guessed correctly – that there would be no shortage of women volunteers coming forward under these conditions. With the removal of Russia

---

88 See Appendix 7.

from the war (although some doctors and nurses stayed in the East),[89] many of the women who had been nurses or drivers[90] of ambulances serving in the East with the Scottish Women's Hospitals, or the Serbian Relief Fund, or with many of the other charitable ambulance and nursing units in the eastern front – Serbia, Romania, Albania, *et al* – were by no means ready to pack up and return home. Not just yet anyway.

Toupie did not waste her time approaching the British Army. The plan was, and most likely always had been, to offer her Unit directly to the service of the Army of the French. However she also anticipated that, even from the French Army, she would face stubborn difficulties, loud disbeliefs, and, not infrequently, sharp masculine antagonism. After the war, in her 1920 Report to the Imperial War Museum, she described her ambition, her pitch both for herself and her women drivers: "to drive an ambulance under…bombardment and shell fire… [undergo] the hardships which field ambulance drivers doing front line work have to undergo."

No doubt after much deep thought, she had forged a clever diplomatic plan, delicately worded. She would present a "petition" requesting "permission" to begin to put together an all women unit – with a dual formation. A Motor Ambulance section, to be commanded by herself… and a Canteen section to be commanded by Miss Norah Hackett. The Motor Ambulance section would naturally supply its own motor cars/ambulances, and when fully assembled would present its potential ambulance services to the Army of the French. And within the contract would be glued a view to carrying out front-line work – under the same conditions as the units staffed by men.

---

89 *Memories of a Doctor in War and Peace*, by Isabel Hutton, CBE, MD pub. Heinemann, 1960, and other accounts.
90 The women in the Hackett Lowthern Unit were always styled as "drivers". Other women ambulance drivers, including the S.W.H. were usually "chauffeurs – or even "chauffeuses".

Norah Hackett, who was to command the Hackett Lowther Canteen section, was already known to the French Army as the Diréctrice of the well-established Women's Emergency Corps Canteen for Soldiers in Compiègne until 1917.[91] The added sweetener of a second Canteen Service, to be managed separately by Miss Hackett, late of the WEC, may well have been diplomatically sewn into Toupie's "petition".[92]

The "petition" was sent to the man currently sitting at the summit of the French army – General Henri Philippe Pétain. And the chances of his agreement were high. General Pétain could hardly turn down any offer of new field ambulance help when large numbers of German troops were expected to start heading in from the east in 1918.[93]

Compiègne, north-east of Paris, was important. It was the terminus of the major railway line from the capital which daily transported surge upon surge of troops new to combat, returning from leave, or wounded and in need of extended hospitalisation. Compiègne would be a major target of the forthcoming German offensive, and the offer of a second canteen for soldiers to be set up could not be lightly refused.

Whether Miss Hackett had already left the WEC voluntarily, or whether she was actively poached by Toupie, will probably

---

91 Not to be confused with the similarly "Women's Emergency Corps" founded in 1914 by Decima Moore and the Hon. Evelina Haverfield with with help from the WSPU. It was later renamed The " Women's Volunteer Reserve."

92 Norah Desmond Hackett (1886–1940) had joined the Women's Emergency Corps (WEC) probably in early 1915. She served in Compiègne as the "Diréctrice" of the local Canteen for Soldiers until sometime in 1917 when there seems to have been a major administrative reorganisation. Earlier in the war, the five staff members of the WEC canteen in Compiègne, as a group, were awarded the Croix de Guerre, which, as the then Diréctrice, Miss Hackett had been chosen to receive and wear. The award is mentioned in a reference from *The British Journal of Nursing 1916* but unfortunately describes no date.

93 See Appendix 7.

never be known. But in her 1920 Report Toupie pays tribute to Miss Hackett:

"My colleague, Miss Desmond Hackett, head of the canteen Section, with her characteristic energy and determination, after endless trouble, through the agency and kind help of Lord Esher and General Clive... got my petition through to General Pétain... wherein I begged that in return for a section which I proposed to raise of twenty cars and thirty-five to thirty women drivers, we should be allowed to do front line work under the same conditions as the men's Units."[94]

Miss Norah Hackett and her dog (name unknown). The Croix de Guerre and ribbon can just be seen. Thanks to Paul Handford and David Simkin.

Clearly the addition of Miss Hackett and her long service at Compiègne for the WEC,[95] with the Croix de Guerre neatly pinned on her bosom, would well build up some useful clout that would be appreciated by General Pétain. It took some months of persuasion... but he finally accepted the offer of the double all women Hackett Lowther Canteen and Ambulance Unit. And most likely never regretted his decision.

Back in London there seems to have been no shortage of volunteers, of all ages, for the new Hackett Lowther Unit. The contract to serve with the Unit was for six months (renewable); the drivers from wealthy families able to provide their own

---

94 Toupie Lowther, 1920 "Report to The Red Cross" held at the Imperial War Museum.
95 Ref: "The Work of the Women's Emergency Corps" in France, compiled by Josephine Davies. Only one copy seems to remain and is in the care of the British Library.

vehicle began to arrive; and Toupie's friends and relatives were tapped to donate ambulances – with the name of the donor proudly painted on the side of course. No few women drivers, many just back home from serving on the east – not to mention the odd American – were eagerly volunteering and were quickly signed up.

It took three months to pull everything together. Drivers recruited, travel documents obtained, uniforms designed and tailored, vehicles gathered and serviced. In January 1918 most of the Hackett Lowther Unit at last all came together and crossed the channel – no doubt all in apple-pie order. They arrived in France with high expectations and seriously looking forward to getting up close and probably uncomfortable at the front.

Toupie in Uniform. With thanks to "L'Escrime et le Tir," October 1923.

10

THE HACKETT LOWTHER UNIT GOES TO WAR 1918-19

The Hackett Lowther Unit was incorporated into the French Army as part of the newly formed Section de Sanitaire, and was to be known as S.S.Y.3 (also written as S.S.3 Y.) attached to the I.P.S.A.E. – "Inspection Permanent, Section Arrierè Region Est." The Unit was now, broadly, part of the whole Army of the French – but not yet attached permanently to any particular individual "Army". This did not please Toupie at the time, but in the months to come, when the Unit had proved its worth and gained its valiant reputation, would happily enable the Unit to hop from one individual "Army" to another, as required.

The drivers were ranked as private soldiers (poilus) and received the by no means generous five sous a day pay. Toupie and Norah Hackett were commissioned as Sous Lieutenants – the equivalent of 2nd Lieutenants in the British Army – at ten sous a day and with one double stripe boldly on the sleeve (un galon sur la manche). Seemingly Miss Hackett, for reasons not quite known but possibly something to do with her service with the WEC, sported a double galon on her tunic sleeve, which did not go down very well.

The drivers were women of all ages, and most knew what they were doing behind the wheel, under the bonnet and with anything connected with tyres. If a driver did not know the ropes when she arrived then she soon did – or went off home. The uniform seems to have been not unhandsome, with a tunic and the usual heavy skirt:

"Coats like British officers' tunics with big square pockets and a leather belt. Skirts coming below the knees, breeches underneath and big high trench boots with thick soles... claret-coloured collars with the automobile grenade signs of the French Army and a special cap... big trench coats such as the officers wear. Mackintosh outside with a detachable fleece lining... shirts are men's, flannel with ordinary soft collar and silk tie, all khaki colour. Fur lined gauntlets, waterproof gloves, waterproof boots... flannel pyjamas and bed-socks."[96]

It was by no means what we would consider to be ideal nowadays, when its wearer often had to scramble in and out of heavy motor vehicles, lift cumbersome bonnets to keep the engines roaring and stem the petrol flowing through the carburettor, – not to say anything of hauling the wounded up and into the ambulance – but no one seems to have complained. Some women elsewhere – the Hector Munro Ambulance Unit[97] for example – did wear breeches with handsomely laced-up gaiters under a short knee length tunic.[98]

A sous Lieutenant, M. Victor Chatenay, was appointed as the liaison officer between the Hackett Lowther Unit and the French Army. Now bordering on thirty years old, he had served in the French Army from the beginning of the war. After being badly wounded in 1917, he was re-

---

96 Quoted from Mary Dexter "In the Soldier's Service", War Experiences – England-Belgium-France 1918.
97 Dr Hector Munro, a director of the Medico-Psychological Clinic in London. put together an Ambulance Unit for work in Belgium in August 1914. Both men and women drivers volunteered.
98 Which became a uniform handsomely re-invented by Vita Sackville-West some years later as ideal gardening gear for women.

posted as a non-combatant and assigned as liaison officer and administrator to the British All Women Unit and Sous Lt Toupie Lowther. This appointment would not by any means have been his first choice, but as an officer and a gentleman he determined, gallantly, to do his best for his "Mesdames". He became responsible for locating billets, as required, the issue of gas masks and blankets, and locating and obtaining adequate supplies of petrol, tools and lamps. And, of course, directing and completing the ceaseless incoming and outgoing paperwork, as well as supervising his own staff: the "maréchal des logis", who acted as secretary and his personal driver, the "auto mechaniques", and the cook. And making sure that Miss Lowther, as he always referred to her, managed the day-to-day organisation, direction, and discipline of the women drivers.

The complete Ambulance section was initially made up of drivers and a fleet of twenty to thirty ambulances, painted grey with a red cross and the name of the donor on the side if appropriate. Some of the ambulances were heavy commercial vehicles, others were large cars that had had a canvas roof added. Seats were taken out to make room for stretchers, and the target was that all the ambulances should carry at least seven *blessés*: four on stretchers in the back and two or three who would ride seated in the front with the driver. Toupie drove her own six-cylinder Wolseley, and there was a Vauxhall, a Chalmers, a Mercedes, a Daimler and a GMC, among others. Toupie's brother Claude, their cousin the 5th Earl of Lonsdale, as well as the Vicomtesse de Breteuil were among the donors, as was the driver Mary Dexter. Toupie's friend of many years, Mlle Gabrielle de Montgeon of Eastington Hall in Worcestershire also joined up and donated an ambulance: she and her housekeeper/companion, Frances Donisthorpe (who had already tasted ambulance work with Evelina Haverfield and the Scottish Women's Hospitals in Serbia) were designated "sous commandants" – second-in-command to Toupie.

On Wednesday, 23rd January 1918, a column of imposing and heavy vehicles, with a military precision, moved in stately convoy out of Paris, arriving two days later at Compiègne. The Unit was to work out of the town of Creil in the Département de l'Oise: Creil and its casualty clearing hospital, the Hôpital de l'Evacuation, was known as station 16.

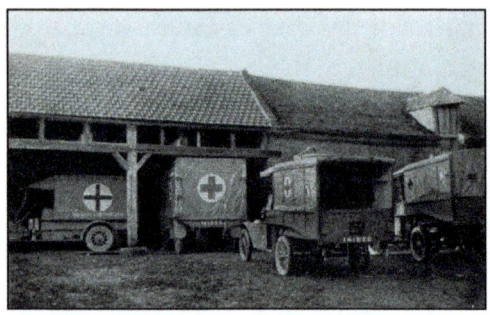

Some Hackett Lowther ambulances; thanks to the unknown photographer.

A handsome billet was splendidly located by Lt Chatenay at the nearby Château de la Vallée. This billet was the first of what would be probably twelve more moves – "déménagements" – before the war's end.

Initially the Unit worked for three months around Creil, station sixteen. The drivers collected casualties from local army hospitals and delivered them to the railway station for evacuation by hospital train to larger, more permanent hospitals. A worthy cause yes, but this was not at all what Toupie had had in mind. This was not serving "under... bombardment and shell fire... doing front line work".

But a great change was on its way. Toupie's wish for the Unit to see active service would soon be more than fulfilled, up to the brim, indeed, and running over. On 21 March, the long-anticipated German offensive of 1918 – the "Ludendorff Offensive" or the "Kaiserschlacht" – (the Kaiser's Battle) – was ready to begin.[99] And suddenly the Hackett Lowther Unit was in the right place at the right time. "Operation Gneisenau", its soldiers, guns, planes, bombs, shells, and gas, was on its way and heading straight towards Compiègne. And after much insisting, and indeed complaining, to the French army top brass, Toupie managed to manoevre the Unit into the 2nd Corps of the French Third Army under General Humbert and the Unit was to stand ready to head towards the battle zone.

With this news, Lt Chatenay sharply ordered a full inspection of the Unit. Tyres, stretchers, and gas masks were checked for use and counted. Any chocolates and cigarettes located in some of the gas mask boxes were ordered to be hastily removed.

Initially the French army fell back, and the Hackett Lowther Unit with it. Lt Chatenay had his hands full when he had to find new billets for the women – not always easy and rarely turning out to be comfortable. The drivers found themselves snatching sleep in dug-outs and cellars, gas masks were ordered to be always at the ready, and heavy blankets had to be stuffed around ill-fitting cellar doors.

No baths, no change of clothing, little sleep and only sardine sandwiches to eat if you were lucky. Maps had become useless, but the Unit knew what to do, did not flinch, and kept going where and when it was ordered. Of the documents that have survived recounting the experience of some of the women drivers, there is not one mention of any driver who "let the side down".

Relatives at home were most likely not told too much: of villages that had descended into broken brick walls, shell craters, and hollow walls crowned by stacked and shattered slates, as the German army, firing all the while, grimly

---

99 There were four major German offensives into France from 21 March–18 July 1918, codenamed Michael, Georgette, Gneisenau and Blücher-Yorck. See Appendix 7.

Katherine Hodges and Toupie in a poste. Thanks to Paul Handford.

advanced. The ambulance drivers, heading to the advanced dressing stations behind an active and falling-back front line, picked up and took away the wounded. All the while dodging the overhead whine of enemy aeroplanes, with pilots ready and able to drop a bomb at any light or movement. Slowly crawling along what was left of the unsignposted and shattered roads.

Katherine Hodges describes:

"At Pimprez the night before last we were gas shelled all night, had to wear our gas masks for five hours. Perfectly awful, you feel you can't breathe in the beastly things. I was standing talking in the evening to a soldier in front of my car and the nightly hymn of hate (the German shelling and bombing) at the other end of the village when suddenly Whizz Crash and a 210 (very large shell) burst about six hundred yards away in an orchard. There was a perfect shower of fragments of shell, and a bit the size of a nut hit my shoulder, but only bruised it. I retired to the dug-out quickly, accompanied by my soldier friend. They plunked them over for about two hours. Fortunately there were no wounded to be taken at the moment so one could stay in the dug-out. They are very good about not sending you out under bombardment unless it is very pressing."[100]

But, at last, the great and bloody tide of the whole Ludendorff Offensive into France started to run out of steam, and

---

[100] Quoted directly from Katherine Hodges' Memorial, unpublished, held at Leeds Library and IWM. Ref: Copyright, Designs and Patents Act 1988 as a Fair Dealing quotation.

"Operation Gneisenau" had ground to a halt just before reaching Compiègne. And Lt Chatenay received an order from "on high" that the exhausted but triumphant – and very proud of itself – Hackett Lowther Unit was to stand down.

The Unit's determined and courageous efforts during the German advance had been exemplary, and had been noticed. On 18th June at the magnificent Château de Fayel, where a new billet had been happily located, Lt Chatenay, Toupie and members of the Unit were decorated with the Croix de Guerre Bronze star, with the right to display a fanion (a small flag) depicting the Croix de Guerre medal on the side of the ambulances. Colonel Meyer – the "Directeur du Service de Santé" – did the honours, and as he did so an aeroplane from the nearby aerodrome swooped around in salute overhead.

However, the order to stand down was not at all what Toupie had in mind. The German advance of 1918, "Gneisenau", may indeed have been halted and then pushed back by the French army under General Mangin, but the war was by no means over. At Toupie's special request, in August 1918, the Hackett Lowther Unit was re-attached to the now advancing 1st French Army "so that we might remain at the front".[101]

The Hackett Lowther Unit quickly jumped back into battle mode. The German army may well have been retreating, but it was fighting as hard as ever it did with bomb, shell, and gas. And again there were villages left with no more than a few bricks standing, churches pulverized, and graves torn up and scattered. Trees fallen, bridges broken, roads treacherous with cracks and cavities. Dead and wounded horses on the sides of the torn roads, wells deliberately poisoned. And dead men still, in shredded uniforms, on all sides. The end, however, was in sight, and not unsurprisingly no few of the Unit's

---

101 Toupie Lowther Report held at the IWM. One can only imagine that the previous performance of the Unit under fire during the Gneisenau advance would have neutralised any lingering objection.

From an "Unattributed" Collection held at the IWM. Toupie's writing can be clearly identified on the back of the photos so they may well have been part of her donation to the IWM in 1920. The rather splendid Château de Fayel, which is still standing, can be clearly seen in the background. Reproduced by permission of the IWM.

drivers scrabbled for desirable German helmets and weapons as souvenirs.

A mighty Allied advance now pressed towards Germany across the line of the now retreating Ludendorff Offensive. British, Portuguese, and American armies all successfully pushed back the now exhausted, and almost defeated, but still-fighting German army.

But, finally, enough had become enough. At last the German High Command bitterly capitulated and the fighting stopped. The war in Europe was over: the Hackett Lowther Unit had served, survived, and could now go home.

During these final hostilities the Unit was twice mentioned in dispatches. A second formal and very smart ceremony occurred on 24th September 1918, when General Fonclare of the 15th Corps happily handed out more Croix de Guerre medals to Toupie and the remaining members of the Unit. The actual Armistice was signed on 11th November 1918.

General Fonclare handing out medals. Photographer unknown.

The Film

In September 1918 a short film which includes both the Hackett and the Lowther tiers of the Unit was put together by the French authorities. Silent, in black and white and lasting some fifteen minutes, the film has been digitally remastered and is available from ECPAD.[102] Both Miss Hackett and Toupie feature. A few still images clearly taken on the same day as the Unit filming also appeared in the magazine *Le Monde Illustré* 7th September 1918

After the Armistice

When the war had come to a halt the Hackett Lowther Unit was invited to go to the French town of Metz to celebrate the longed-for return of the province of Lorraine to France. The Unit continued to keep themselves busy by working for a big hospital outside the town during the day, with enjoyable evenings spent on welcome sociable entertainments. There

---
102 Etablissement de Communication et de Production Audiovisuelle de la Défense: Item 14.18. A 853

were balls and dances, both with and without fancy dress, and colours and evening costumes were imaginatively put together. And, not least, there were numbers and numbers of French officers – of all ranks and of all ages, possibly married, possibly not – all eager and ready to be very appreciative of the women of the Unit. Lt. Chatenay, although clearly pleased, but nevertheless always aware of his dignity, wrote in his diary that he felt obliged to keep a certain distance from these festivities: he did not want at all to be compared to a director of a "corps de ballet".

A few of the drivers, no doubt with mixed feelings, were now drifting away from the Unit to head back to England. However, the most highly desirable honour was to follow: in January 1919 the Hackett Lowther Ambulance Unit was invited to travel into Germany as part of the occupying Army of France and alongside General Mangin's Tenth Army. Naturally Toupie gladly accepted the invitation, and the Hackett Lowther Unit, along with Lt Chatenay, had a wintery drive through deep snow, not without humorous incident, to the old German city of Wiesbaden. Another six weeks of fine entertainment followed, with balls and dances every evening and innumerable French officers ready and available to dance until dawn.

Until, at last, it really was time to go home.

At Wiesbaden in 1919. Toupie in full kit wearing the Croix de Guerre with an unknown high-ranking French officer. Behind his shoulder, looking at the camera, is Driver Barbara Stirling. Thanks to Paul Handford.

The Hackett Lowther Unit was finally disbanded on 29th March 1919, when the Great War was officially ended in a railway carriage at Compiègne in France. Although during the course of the war some of the drivers had left the Unit, either because they had come to the end of their contract or from ill health – or even from a desire to do so – not one had been wounded in action.

Lt Victor Chatenay stayed with the Unit until it was finally disbanded. At first he had struggled with the blithe tendency of his English ladies to ignore army discipline and instruction, but as time passed his emotions had mellowed into admiration and he found himself, on no few occasions, defending and firmly championing his "Mesdames".

Lt Chatenay and Toupie, most likely outside the Château de Fayel. With thanks to Paul Handford.

The Times noted Toupie's return to England:

> **ENGLISHWOMEN WITH THE FRENCH ARMY**
> **MISS TOUPIE LOWTHER'S UNIT**
>
> Lieutenant Toupie Lowther, who with a unit of Englishwomen took part in the front line work of the French Army… is now back in London again her unit having been disbanded. The yellow fanion of her corps with the cock of France on one corner and the lion of England on the other hangs in her home.

All of the women of the Hackett Lowther Unit who served in France at the at the time of the Armistice, were eligible for the Victory and the British War medals.

The Victory and War medals

The Croix de Guerre

II

THE TROUBRIDGE DIARIES

Toupie's other diary appearances are in the far more infamous, even venomous, diaries and journals of Una Troubridge.[103] Early entries describe Toupie as a new and endearing friend – somewhat eccentric in dress but useful for supplying driving lessons and throwing the odd party. But as time drifts by, the entries slide towards the critical, and finally into the downright hostile.

Una Troubridge's diaries, later known as "day books" (and after John/Marguerite Radclyffe Hall's death as "Letters to John") are currently held across the Atlantic, some in Canada and others in the USA: both it would seem in no wonderful condition. Toupie's appearances in the Troubridge diaries are not infrequent after the Great War ended, but by no means with any lengthy description of her life interestingly attached. So on approaching this particular chapter it was sensible to rely almost

---

103 Margot Elena Gertrude Taylor (1887–1963), who was always known as Una, had married Ernest Troubridge in 1908. When Troubridge was knighted in 1919, Una could have, and probably did in earlier days, rightly style herself Lady Ernest Troubridge. When they subsequently separated they did not divorce, as both were Catholics; consequently, Una retained her right to be so styled – with a minor variation, until her own death.

entirely upon previous biographers to lead me to, and thus to comment upon, her movements in and out of the Troubridge narrative. I admit to owing a great debt of gratitude to all of those talented writers and their valiant researchers who have gone before, and whose footsteps I have followed. But I claim no obligation to agree with any previously published conclusions.

Marguerite Radclyffe Hall – soon to be rather undramatically renamed as "John" or "Johnnie" – had taken up with Mabel Batten around about 1908. Both had, without any doubt, known Toupie for some years. Toupie's reaction to the circumstances that overlaid Mabel's sadly unpleasant death in 1916, the second year of the war, however, remains unknown.

After the launch of the Hall/Troubridge partnership, Toupie does appear fairly frequently in the entries of Una Troubridge's diaries that describe serious post-war socialising. They give a cheerful portrait of heady social activity – visiting, partying, clubbing, theatre visits, shared weekends and shopping. Toupie appears along with a multitude of other like-minded women, some of whom had also served in the war, and whose loyalty over the still-to-come verdict of "obscene libel" against *The Well of Loneliness* in 1928 would be much tested.

In 1920, when John and Una moved into their new house Chip Chase in Hadley Wood, Hertfordshire, Toupie paid them a visit and was very much "in favour". "John and Una thought her a dear, they were amused by the imitation flowers she wore in her buttonhole and Una started work on a bust of Toupie in her uniform intended for the Imperial War Museum."[104]

The friendship and weekends at Chip Chase continued, expanded even, and it would seem very likely that it was through Toupie and her – nowadays best-referred to as

---

104 Quoted by Michael Baker in *Our Three Selves*. The house then "Chip Chase" is still there. It was virtually rebuilt and enormously extended in 2006 and renamed Camlet Corner. Thanks to John Leatherdale and the Hadley Wood Association.

friendship circles – that Una, and the now permanently renamed John, were introduced to many new and interesting acquaintances and their social life started to bloom. There was a few days' holiday in sunny Brighton and a visit to Toupie's brother Claude – still an MP, and always busy restoring his handsome Herstmonceux Castle in west Sussex.

However, rumbling in the background during the later months of 1920 was the very public victory of John's action for slander against St. George Lane Fox-Pitt, who had, in anger, described her to the secretary of the Society for Psychical Research as "a thoroughly immoral woman". And offering a supportive opinion from Una's now long-abandoned husband, Sir Ernest Troubridge. The court graciously awarded John £500 in damages, and the newspapers picked up a plentiful selection of colourful and dramatic copy and headlines.

Fox-Pitt then appealed against the verdict. Successfully but to little advantage either to his pocket or his reputation.

John, although angrily wanting a retrial, reluctantly followed the stern advice from her lawyer: advice that contained a double-edged message. "Her character had been more than cleared" she was advised, "and it would be futile spending much money and having more odious publicity when Fox Pitt would never pay a penny".

What she seemingly took no heed of was any future fall-out from her victory: that although she had won £500 in damages, she had been publicly tagged as a practitioner of sexual immorality, gross indecency and serious unchastity. And that some unwelcome writing might still be simmering on the wall.[105]

---

105 The tag did not go away. In 1921, Frederick Alexander Macquisten, a Unionist MP for Glasgow Springburn, was so enraged that he promptly upped and proposed to the House of Commons that a clause, "Acts of Gross indecency by females", should be added to the Criminal Law Amendent Act, which had in 1895 propelled Oscar Wilde into his two years in Reading Gaol. The clause was passed in the Commons but was defeated in the House of Lords.

Toupie may well have not been at all impressed by this public rumble and rumour, John's victory notwithstanding. The newspapers had always been kind to her: always happy to trumpet her sporting successes – even her near misses on the tennis court – as well as the months in France with the Hackett Lowther Ambulance Unit. But of her private life, nothing had ever been said.

John and Una, heartily pushed St George Fox-Pitt to one side. The twenties were roaring in, and in 1921 Chip Chase was sold and the couple moved from distant and rural Hertfordshire to booming post-war London. Where, of course, all the social action was now to be found, and there was plenty of it.

A new circle of acquaintances, still relying much on Toupie's "salon", appears in the Troubridge diaries: women writers, women musicians, and a comfortable round of almost permanent young and not-so-young party-timers. Some who worked, some who did not. And some were from the days in France.

With the war not that long over, Una records a Hackett Lowther reunion with Enid Elliott (daughter of General Edward Locke Elliott) and the Hon. Eileen Plunket (daughter of Lord Plunket, an Irish peer). Both were ambulance drivers from the Unit: both later married. Along with "Honey" (Pamela Veronica Harris Austin, grand-daughter of Mabel Batten) and a "Poppy" (yet to be identified) as well as Gabrielle de Montgeon and Nellie Rowe, the Australian singer and teacher. There was also company of the theatrical and bookish kind: Gwen Farrar (1899–1944), actress, singer and cello player; Teddie Gerard (1880–1942), actress; Tallulah Bankhead (1902–68), actress and film star; Ida Wylie (1885–1959), writer and novelist; May Sinclair (1863–1946), also a writer and novelist; as well as Vere Hutchinson (1891–1932), a novelist; and Gabrielle

Enthoven (1868–1950), actress, producer and director. And a merry company of others. Deeds and names fly backwards and forwards in the old tradition of lunches at the Savoy and the Hyde Park Grill: afternoon teas continue happily, followed by night-time visits to bohemian clubs in London. There is much dancing at the Cave of Harmony, the Hambone Club and the Orange Tree Club – all wickedly fashionable and dubiously catering to the jazz age: artistic and musical working women, writers, poets and actors alongside drifters from the upper classes and a surfeit of alcohol and, probably, cocaine.

In 1921 the artist Romaine Brooks appeared in London, and Toupie seems to have given a party for her. However problems followed. In her diary Una writes that Toupie became infatuated with Romaine, "who encouraged her advances then treated her coldly", and Toupie is reported as becoming increasingly quarrelsome because she had not been invited to visit Brooks in Capri. As a result John and Una cancelled their own visit.[106]

This version of the whole episode, looking at it now, seems a dull, tedious, very minor event that does not really ring true. There is another version from the biographer of Romaine Brooks, Meryle Secrest, who presents a differing view of this stormy teacup. Now it is Romaine herself who has invited Toupie, as a friend of "Una and Johnnie's", to the party at the request of her – Romaine's – lover, Natalie Barney, but Toupie declined:

"I only asked T. because you wanted me to do so. I knew that I should be exposing myself to some silly disagreeable misunderstand by inviting T... Why give second-rate conceited people the occasion of showing their silly fangs... I asked to know [be introduced to] May Sinclair and [Johnnie's]

---
106 Quoted from *Radclyffe Hall, a Woman called John* by Sally Cline (Faber & Faber, 1997).

answer was when she came back [from her cure]! Now Lady T. intends seeing you in Paris, of course you must do as you want etc."[107]

The chilly reference to Toupie as "Lady T." can be either mocking – which is most likely – or venomous, indicating a sour knowledge of her father's illegitimacy, but this is not really likely.

On a better note socially, there were trips to Paris and visits to Natalie Barney and her literary, artistic and musical haute-monde "salon" on Fridays at 22 Rue Jacob. Toupie and Natalie had known each other for years – they had been to the same school in France[108] and were both equally fluent in the French language. It has to be no surprise that Toupie, the Croix-de-Guerre holder, composer and one-time serious sportsperson would have long been a long term member of such a Salon.

A multitude of Natalie Barney's guests and visitors have been recorded on a hand-drawn cartoon, boldly titled "Le Salon de l'Amazon".[109] The cartoon is a glorious muddle of names of the bright, the clever, the literary, the musical and the artistic (and frequently aristocratic) visitors of all sexes who visited Natalie's "Temple of Friendship". Not unsurprisingly, the name "T. Lowther" is boldly stamped in the top left-hand quadrant; upside down at the base of the drawing are included the names "Lady Troubridge and Radclyffe Hall"

After the successful trial for slander against St John Lane Fox-Pitt in 1920, Marguerite Radclyffe Hall docked both "Marguerite" and "John" from her name, abandoned poetry, and began to put pen to paper under an ambiguous – but by no means unfashionable – nom-de-plume, "Radclyffe Hall". Her career as a popular writer leapt into life, her books sold

---

107 A letter from Romaine Brooks to Natalie Barney, quoted *in Between Me and Life: a Biography of Romaine Brooks*, by Meryl Secrest (Pub. Macdonald and Jane's, 1976).
108 6 See Chapter 5.
109 Reproduced in Appendix 11.

well and in 1926 *Adam's Breed* received "The James Tait Black Memorial Prize". Public esteem was clearly gathering pace and confident in this new career as a well-known and very popular modern novelist with a fine reputation, Radclyffe Hall now planned a leap into the unknown. To write deeply and emotionally of the life and the loves of one outstanding character: one of the so many silent women who love only other women, and to include in the narrative a dramatic look back to the Great War now safely ten years in the past. Her heroine would be given the fully masculine name "Stephen Gordon", and, in time of war, serve in wartime France with an all women ambulance unit. And find there her happiness and her life's companion. Detail and description of driving an ambulance in France during the war, would, of course, be obtainable very easily from those who had actually been there, and the book would be gifted with a grim but very catching title, *The Well of Loneliness*.

Radclyffe Hall was seemingly unconcerned that a slumbering memory of the Fox-Pitt slander trial of 1920, if prodded, would suddenly wake up and rear itself inside many morally-minded minds. And indeed almost as soon as *The Well of Loneliness* was published in July 1928, the newspapers and other critical publications were instantly ablaze. Moral knives were sharpened, dire punishments were threatened, and old wounds horribly ripped open. *The Well* suffered a trial for obscenity in November 1928: Sir Chartres Biron was the presiding magistrate. Now officially deemed an "obscene libel" *The Well* was banned from publication in the UK and all copies were ordered to be burned.[110]

As a novelist Radclyffe Hall, had never been averse to stitching real life into her fiction and, there is not the least doubt that the Hackett Lowther Unit was her source for the all women Breakspeare Ambulance Unit. However of the

---

110 But not those in the USA.

members of the Breakspeare Unit and Stephen Gordon she had included a delicate description:[111]

"... and amongst them there were those even as she."[112]

And the summing up words of Sir Chartres Biron, quoted in no few newspapers, were very clear:

"... according to the writer of this book, a number of women of position and admirable character, who were engaged in driving ambulances in the course of the war, were addicted to this vice."

After Sir Chartres Biron's ugly comment and the verdict of "obscene libel", the friendship years between Toupie and the Hall-Troubridge duo disintegrated and did not ever recover. Which is not surprising.

After Toupie's death in 1944, Una struck back. In her tearful biography *The Life and Death of Radclyffe Hall*, written in 1945 but not published until 1961, she writes:

"A strange creature she [Toupie] was, a remarkable athlete who did fine work in the First World War. But she was essentially a crank. A compound of the very male and very feminine. She passed out of our lives when John wrote *The Well of Loneliness*, and we afterwards heard that she had resented the book as challenging her claim to be the only invert in existence. Later still, when she was growing very old, I was told that she had moreover acquired the illusion that she had served as a model for Stephen Gordon."[113]

Whilst her book *The Life and Death of Radclyffe Hall*, was being put together, Una had launched a flux of letter-writing to many of their one-time friends, probably searching for interesting recollections and pithy items that could be included. In 1944 she wrote to Toupie, now facing death

---

111 Referring to the women serving with the "Breakspeare Unit".
112 Quoted from *The Well of Loneliness*.
113 Una, Lady Troubridge, *The Life and Death of Radclyffe Hall*, 1945. Pub. 1961 by the Citadel Press, New York.

from tuberculosis, and who in return invited Una to visit at her home in Pulborough, West Sussex. The visit was not a success.[114]

Una Troubridge and John Radclyffe Hall at a dog show – one of their favourite occupations., probably 1930s, both seemingly in neither good humour nor tip-top health. Names of dogs unknown. With thanks to TopFoto, www.topfoto.co.uk

---

114 Her description of the visit also contains a hefty chunk of bad mouthing of Toupie's god-daughter, Fabienne Brethous-Lafargue. For more unpleasant detail see Chapter 13.

12

A FEW OTHER FRIENDS

Fragments and names of other friends and acquaintances appear in the records of Toupie's life, mostly without a great deal of description of personality or even convincing identification. Surnames are invariably not present. Toupie appears to have been a woman who "knew everybody". No doubt a book that described all of Toupie's friends would end up as large as the complete works of William Shakespeare. Una Troubridge's diaries are a major source of identification of other friends: some overlap, and some, on closer examination, do not.

Mademoiselle Gabrielle Marie Alice de Montgeon

Gabrielle Marie Alice was the daughter of M. Amédée de Cavelier de Montgeon, a member of the ancient and very noble family of the counts of de Montgeon of Normandy, and his American wife, Alice, daughter of John A. Post (then, and now, a very prominent American family). Her father died, aged twenty-nine, in June 1876 when little Gabrielle was just six months old, leaving her a very rich baby. Indeed, all of her life Gabrielle was a wealthy woman: her father had provided for the daughter he had barely come to know most handsomely in his will. That he would have seen his daughter in her cradle before his early death is somehow comforting.

Gabrielle de Montgeon and much information with thanks to Shirley Carr and Susan Harland, Mlle. de Montgeon's great nieces.

Gabrielle's mother, Alice de Montgeon, later married Mariano de Cuadra, and another daughter, Lili, was born. Gabrielle and her "new" family became close – Lili married an Englishman and had a family – and their many descendants have retained fine photographs of Gabrielle de Montgeon. Mariano and Alice de Cuadra are buried in Longdon Churchyard near Eastington Hall in Worcestershire, where there is a memorial.

A wealthy woman, Gabrielle, always known as Mlle de Montgeon, bought Eastington Hall, Upton on Severn, and lived there until her death in 1944. The Hall was originally an old Tudor house which she set about restoring to a high standard. She seems to have led a fairly quiet life there, possibly farming – she is reported in *The Times* of December 1923, along with Miss Frances Donisthorpe, as winning prizes for pigs at a local country show – interspersed, however, with many visits to London. She seems to have been very close to her half-sister Lili's three children, who are remembered handsomely in her will.

Gabrielle de Montgeon features frequently in Toupie's life as a friend of many years' standing, yet how they first met has not yet come to light. Toupie's mother, Louise, names Gabrielle de Montgeon as an executrix in her will, which is not a position given to a stranger but rather to a trusted, long-term family friend.

Gabrielle de Montgeon: with thanks to Paul Handford.

In her own will Toupie remembers Gabrielle de Montgeon generously. The most probable theory, and indeed most wonderful, of how the two women first met is that they both went to school at Les Ruches.[115] There are only two years between the two, and as a fatherless but wealthy French child (and her mother remarrying), Les Ruches would not be a surprising choice of school for Gabrielle.

Mlle de Montgeon and Frances Donisthorpe both served in the Hackett Lowther Ambulance Unit as "adjointes" (assistant directors) to Toupie.[116] Both donated an ambulance and, presumably, they were out there with the other drivers during times of enemy action as needed, but they may also have helped with the deployment of the drivers – as well as the paperwork. In her "Report to the Red Cross" of 1920, Toupie writes that she is "indebted to the invaluable assistance of Miss Frances Donisthorpe… with her past experience as second in command of Mrs Haverfield's Scottish Women's Rumanian [sic] expedition".[117]

Both Mlle de Montgeon and Miss Donisthorpe stayed with the Unit throughout, and went to Germany at the end of the war.

---

115 See Chapter 5.
116 Chatenay, *Mon journal de Quatorze–Dix-huit*.
117 Toupie's reference to Mrs Haverfield would seem to indicate that Frances Donisthorpe served with The Hon. Evelina Haverfield in a Scottish Women's Hospitals ambulance unit, probably in Serbia. Seemingly until Mrs Haverfield, after a disagreement with Dr Elsie Inglis, left the SWH in March 1917.

Frances Elizabeth Donithorpe

Frances (Fanny) Elizabeth Donisthorpe was born in 1870 into the large family of Alfred R. Donisthorpe and his wife Sarah. He was a rich textile industrialist, and lived with his large family for many years in Coleorton Hall near Ashby-de-la-Zouche, and then in Quenby Hall in Leicestershire.[118] Frances is said to have been an "ardent" follower of Leicestershire's Quorn Hunt, and lived as the "housekeeper" for many years at Eastington Hall with Gabrielle de Montgeon. Gabrielle's nieces and nephew knew her as "Donnie". She did not marry, and died on 19th June 1944 of "cardiovascular degeneration" at Barnwood House Hospital.[119] Her death certificate is signed by G. W. T. H. Fleming, the medical superintendent, and her home is given as Eastington Hall.

Frances Donnisthorpe with thanks to Shirley Carr and Susan Harland.

Mlle Gabrielle de Montgeon also did not marry. She died at Eastington Hall on 1st July 1944, eleven days after Donnie Donisthorpe.

Toupie at Eastington Hall with dogs. Probably post war. Thanks to Paul Handford.

---

118 *Country Life*, 3rd September 1904.
119 Barnwood House Hospital was a private mental hospital in Barnwood, Gloucester.

Nellie Rowe

"Nellie" Rowe, born Helen Lucy Rowe in Melbourne in 1861, was a singer and teacher of music. As a young woman she was a pupil of Mme Mathilde Marchesi (1821–1913) a highly esteemed teacher of operatic and drawing-room singing throughout Europe who was personally acquainted with all the lauded opera composers of the time.[120] After her studies Nellie began her career as a singer, but finding herself suffering from stage fright, she changed tack and became a teacher of music to the rich and famous rather than a performer. She lived and received pupils for many years at her home at 31 Cromwell Road, London (not a million miles away from Toupie in Old Brompton Road), which was frequently used for recitals.

Nellie Rowe and family reminiscence with thanks to Ros Escott.

Nellie Rowe's great-great-niece, Ros Escott, is a family historian and has kindly supplied photos of Nellie and reminiscences.

When relatives visited Nellie in London in 1927... "they were amazed to find that she had lost her Australian accent... she was dressed in mauve to match her drawing room and was stretched out on a "chaise lounge". In the Rowe archives are a number of very warm and friendly letters from the composer Percy Grainger to Cecile Rowe, Nellie's unmarried sister in Australia who "sang nicely but never professionally."

Nellie Rowe and Toupie make several snapshot appearances together in Una Troubridge's diaries – not very unsurprisingly to Nellie's detriment. For example: in 1920 Toupie and Nellie visited John and Una's (then) home, Chip Chase. Toupie

---

120 *Marchesi and Music,* by Mathilde Marchesi: pub. Lightning Source UK Ltd.

would sometimes bring along her dog, Priest, who was popular with John and Una, and sometimes with Nellie Rowe who was not. Then again, all four visited Brighton and Toupie stayed with her mother in Hove whilst John, Una and Nellie were at The Princes Hotel. According to Una, Nellie became offended, left early and went back to London.[121] It is of course much more likely that Nellie simply had a very good reason for going back to London. She was, after all, a professional woman with her own career to maintain.

Nellie Rowe died in a nursing home in London on 30th July 1942, aged eighty-one. She was buried at Maidenhead cemetery after a Requiem Mass at the Brompton Oratory.

Gabrielle Enthoven

In her diaries Una Troubridge mostly uses only first names – surnames are so infrequent as to be hardly visible. And although understandable, this has not been helpful to readers of other Hall/Troubridge biographies.

There were two Gabrielles in Toupie's life (three, if Mme Gabrièle, the French Champion fencer is include): Mlle Gabrielle de Montgeon; and Mrs Gabrielle Enthoven OBE. From time to time this has caused some confusion.

If the address mentioned in the diary entry – perhaps for a weekend in the deep countryside – is Eastington Hall, the Gabrielle will be Mlle de Montgeon. For theatrical performances in London or elsewhere, the Gabrielle will probably be Augusta Gabrielle Enthoven, née Romaine (1868–1950), a well-known and highly-regarded woman of the theatre. This Gabrielle was a writer, producer, and actor, a friend of the theatrical stars in the London of the 1920s as well as the Hollywood stars across

---

121 *Radclyffe Hall: A Woman Called John*, by Sally Cline (Faber & Faber, 1997).

the water in 1930s Hollywood. She married a Major Charles Enthoven in 1893, and her name can be found in many books and websites dedicated to the theatre over the years. She was also a friend of Mabel Batten – no surprise there.

Gabrielle Enthoven had a major clash with Una Troubridge. Una had written a stage version of the French writer Colette's well known and bestselling novel *Chéri*, and Gabrielle Enthoven had been roped in to stage, produce, and play the lead.[122] Good reviews from the press were anticipated and good audiences expected. As well as some theatrical praise for the author, could a new career possibly be on its way? However, the play turned out to be a miserable failure and seems to have closed rapidly after its initial London performance. Naturally, the producer and lead player, Gabrielle Enthoven, was held to blame: and, as to be expected, any potential further social intimacy between John, Una and Mrs Enthoven was instantly abolished.

A phenomenally well-known and much admired theatrical personality, Gabrielle Enthoven was also an avid collector of playbills, prints, books, engravings, memorabilia and many more items of rare and artistic theatre history which, after her death, were (and still are) housed in the V&A Museum.

Mrs. Enthoven was for many years also acquainted with the ladies of Smallhythe near Rye in East Sussex – Edith "Edy" Craig, Clare "Tony" Atwood and Christabel Marshall (Christopher St. John) – and their theatre.

She is said to have donated a portrait photograph of Sir Henry Drummond Wolff[123] – the ambassador in Madrid whom Claude Lowther first worked for as attaché – to the National Portrait Gallery, date unknown.

---

122 Sadly date unknown.
123 See Appendix 8.

13

FABIENNE BRETHOUS-LAFARGUE

As has already been said, Toupie Lowther was one of those people who knows – and is known to – everybody. References to her presence at a sporting or theatrical activity, or in letters from a member of some artistic or titled family, appear frequently. However, caution suggests that these glimpses are by no means indicative of a stunning window into a life-long friendship. The diaries of Una Troubridge contain a rather unpleasant rendering of Toupie's relationship to "Fabienne", most likely based entirely on guesswork and malice, showing no insight into their real relationship. Fabienne D'Avilla features in Toupie's will as a major beneficiary and is described by Toupie quite simply as "my God-child". There is no reason to suppose otherwise.

Fabienne's family long features in Toupie's life. Her father was León Jean-Baptiste Brethous-Lafargue from the Bordeaux region of France. Her mother was an Englishwoman Gertrude Janet Elisabeth Jones-Dussaut, who, after the death of Mlle Caroline Dussaut had become the head teacher of Les Ruches school in Fontainebleau.[124]

M. Brethous-Lafargue seems to have obtained a divorce from his first wife[125] in April 1900, and his marriage to Mlle

---
124 See Chapter 5 "Education".
125 Name unknown. So far no information about this lady has yet been uncovered.

Jones-Dussaut took place in Paris very soon after, on 4th July 1900.

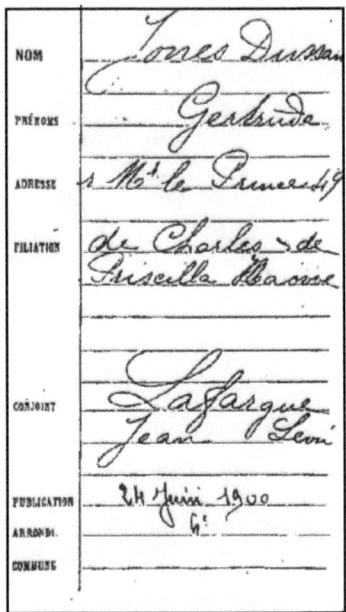

Marriage banns of Jones-Dussaut, Gertrude (her parentage is included) and Lafargue, Jean Léon.[131]

Described as an "homme de letters", he was a writer and a poet and *inter alia* tutor to the highly regarded French composer Ernest Chausson.[126] Interestingly, one of his novels, published earlier in 1887, is entitled "Fabienne": but it is now, rather sadly, out of print, so whether the title reflects his daughter, or whether his daughter was named after the book, may not ever be known. In fact none of his books seem to be currently in print, and none translated into English.

After the marriage Gertrude Brethous-Lafargue née Jones seems to have left Les Ruches, not unsurprisingly, and a daughter, named Fabienne, was born in August 1901; an Entry of Birth is available online. The image has been a little cropped so that the birth registration is just about legible.

The family of Fabienne's mother has yet to be fully identified: a search to locate her original "Jones" family is hampered by the large number of such-named families, and there can be no firmly-known date or place of birth. Gertrude could also have been a favourite name, a second or third, which she used by choice, although Fabienne's Certificate

---

126 1855–1899.
127 Thanks to Marie Françoise Bastit.

of [British] Naturalisation of 1935 does give her mother's forenames as "Gertrude Janet Elizabeth".

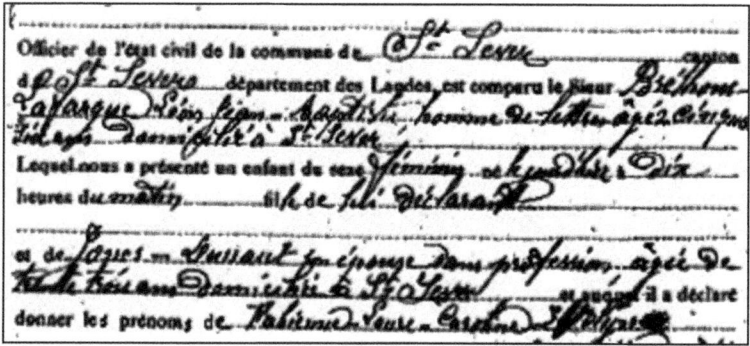

Copy of the Entry of Birth of Fabienne Laura Caroline Evelyn Brethous-Lafargue, born 30*th* August 1901 at the Château des Tourettes, St Sever, Department Landes, France.

The Château des Tourettes is still standing and is in private hands. The building is featured this postcard, dated 1905.

A carte postale depicting the Château des Tourettes, post-marked "St Sever sur l'Adour". It is inscribed "Bons souvenirs voeux affectioneux pour 1905… Gertie, Jean, Fabienne" (Happy remembrances best wishes for 1905).

Toupie would have attended Les Ruches around the time Gertrude Jones-Dussaut took over as proprietor/head teacher after Caroline Dussaut's death in 1887. She would have known Gertrude Jones-Dussaut from Les Ruches, before her marriage to León Jean-Baptiste Brethous-Lafargue and before Fabienne was born, grew up and left France. Clearly it was Fabienne's mother who would have been Toupie's contemporary and who probably invited Toupie to become god-mother to her daughter.

Little can be gleaned about the later life of Mme Gertrude Brethous-Lafargue after her marriage and the birth of her daughter. She outlived Toupie by seven years and had received the bequest of a diamond pin from Toupie's will. Gertrude Brethous-Lafargue 's death has been recorded as occurring in Bordeaux,[128] France on 11th January 1952 in her 81st year which would give her a date of birth of around 1870.[129]

Aged twenty, Fabienne married a Brazilian, Pedro Frederico Vaz de Carvalhaes, and they had a son, Barnabé Raimundo Vaz de Carvalhaes.

The record of Fabienne's marriage has been added onto her birth notification, as was customary in France. It is just about legible in the top left-hand corner.

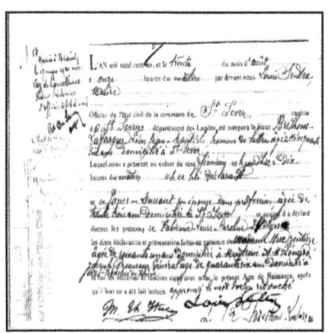

Thanks to Archives Departmental de Seine-et-Marne.

At a time still regretfully unknown, Fabienne de Carvalhaes seemingly abandoned this marriage – both her husband and her child – although she did write to her son from time to time. Barnabé Raimundo grew up in Brazil, married, and has grandchildren living, who, sadly, have little knowledge of their great-grandmother.

Fabienne became a naturalised British citizen on 17th July 1935. In her Certificate of Naturalisation she describes herself as "Fabienne Laura

---

128 Bordeaux may well be the "registration district" of the time. It would seem not unlikely that she died at her home: the Château des Tourettes.
129 Ref. the Andrews Newspaper Index cards.

Evelyn Caroline Brethous-Lafargue d'Avilla", with no reference to her marriage or her child, or to any reason for the addition of another (presumed) surname, d'Avilla. Why this should be so has yet to be uncovered.

In her will Toupie describes Fabienne as her god-child so it would not been surprising that when Fabienne left her first marriage she came to live close to Toupie: in or around the new, handsome and roomy house "Lowther Lodge" in the town of Pulborough, West Sussex. Probably 1935, about the time when the new house was built.

Fabienne Brethous-Lafargue d'Avilla as a young woman, reproduced kind permission from Ada Dawnay.

By this time, now aged over sixty, to Toupie had come to the fate so often suffered by the youngest child of the family: the solitary sibling left alive. To find, in her later life, that she could give a home to her godchild, the daughter of Gertrude Jones-Dussaut, known from schooldays in Fontainbleau long past, would surely be a cause for much happiness. That she would come to be deeply attached to the much younger Fabienne and to come to love her dearly would seem to be both normal, natural and a source of great joy. And not impossibly of no little angst, as so many a parent may come to discover. Paragraph eleven in Toupie's will reads:

"I earnestly entreat the said Fabienne Evelyn Brethous-Lafargue D'Avilla to exercise care and judgment if and when she feels prompted to use part of the four thousand pounds which I have bequeathed to her, and to live on her income."

It is in her will that Toupie refers to Fabienne as her "god-child", and there is no reason to disbelieve that this is anything other than absolutely so. Yet Una Troubridge's apparent view that there was a different kind of relationship between them, and which seeped into her diaries, so far has not been challenged by any of Radclyffe Hall's biographers. Fabienne was twenty-seven years younger than Toupie, which is a mighty gap, and some questioning might well have been successfully researched.

Nevertheless, after New Year's Eve 1924[130] Fabienne does seem to have been regularly introduced to Toupie's friends, mingling happily with the Hall/Troubridge circle. One entry in the Troubridge diaries describes a dinner with "Toupie, Fabienne and Gabrielle".[131] Reporting into her diary afterwards, Una applies the callous description of "hermaphrodite" to Toupie: whatever her appearance or manner this must have been of no consequence to her godchild. It is not unlikely, yet again, to be a rancid swipe from the prime author of unsavoury imaginations.

When John and Una take a trip to France in 1926 they stop off in Paris and have dinner with Toupie and Fabienne, going on to the theatre to see Édouard Bourdet's play *La Prisonnière*[132], a play recounting the love affair between Violet Trefusis and Winnaretta Singer (later to become the Princess de Polignac). They also visit Colette and Natalie Barney, meet the actress Eva Le Gallienne, as well as the Duchesse de Clermont Tonnerre and Mimi Franchetti.[133] None of which is any surprise. Visiting Paris to see old friends would be most likely routine: Fabienne, born in France, clearly a French speaker, would not be anything but highly welcomed by Natalie Barney and her ever-lengthening skeins of both historical and modern friendship.

---

130 From Diana Souhami, *The Trials of Radclyffe Hall* (pub. Weidenfeld & Nicolson, 1998).
131 Surely Gabrielle de Montgeon.
132 *La Prisonnière* was translated by Gilbert Wakefield and also shown in London at the Arts Theatre in November 1927, then repeated in 1930. It was also shown in Germany and the USA.
133 One time lover of Natalie Barney and most likely the source of the leading figure in Compton Mackenzie's 1928 novel *Extraordinary Women*.

And who, of course, with her sister Laura, as previous pupils at Les Ruches, would have known and remembered Fabienne's mother, Mlle Gertrude Dussaut-Jones.

It would be impossible to improve on Diana Souhami's rendering of Una Troubridge's savage account of her visit to Toupie after Radclyffe Hall's death in 1943. "Toupie", Una wrote, "railed at God from her bedroom window for taking her wife Fabienne from her." Fabienne is described now as "Tough, promiscuous, cruel…, living with her amant de cour, Liza, in a nearby cottage owned by Toupie. They were waiting for Toupie to die so as to scoop her inheritance. Una was not going near".[134]

The accuracy of this interpretation of circumstances is, of course, open to oceanically-deep questioning. Toupie had long fallen into disfavor with Una Troubridge – whose emotional balance after John's death and the final years savagely warped by John's infatuation for the young Russian émigré Evguenia Souline – cannot in any way be relied upon.

"Liza" seems to be Elizabeth Sophia Wolfe. As a young woman she was a well-known squash player, and was played annually between the women's squash associations of the UK and the USA. Her son, Gerald Heygate Wolfe, was Fabienne's godson.

Fabienne's application to join the P.E.N. "English Centre",[135] alongside Mrs Elizabeth S. F. Wolfe, gives an address of Rose Cottage, Sutton, Pulborough, Sussex and describes her occupation as novelist/writer. A later address gives Orchard Twitten, Nutbourne Pulborough.

If asked later Fabienne always described herself as a "writer". Under the name Francis D'Avilla she seems to have published two books of poetry in French: *La Coupe d'Abatre*

---

134 Quoted from *The Trials of Radclyffe Hall*, by Diana Souhami.
135 Poets, Essayists, Novelists. See online for details of P.E.N. International.

pub. Editions de la Jeune Academie 1929 and *Sous les Etoiles* (pub. Albert Messein 1937). She also translated Lord Alfred Douglas' *Poems* into French (also pub: Albert Meissen 1937).

As Evelyn Fabyan In the popular paperback series of the 1950 *The Ghost Book*, there are three of her short stories. In the Second Ghost book, "Bombers Night", in the Third Ghost book "Napoleon's Hat"[136] and in the Fourth Ghost book "The Lorraine Cross".

On 7th August 1945, Fabienne married Major Jack Montagu Hillyard, the son of George and Blanche Hillyard, Toupie's tennis friends for many years – now near neighbours in Nutbourne on the edges of Pulborough.[137] He was fifty-four and she forty-two. Liza Heygate was a witness at the marriage, which took place at the Westminster Registry Office in London. During the Great War Jack Hillyard had served in the Royal Artillery, and he maintained that his lack of success as a tennis player – compared to that of his parents – was because of his time in the army during the war.

They were divorced in 1954. Jack Hillyard went to live in Ireland, where he married again, this time Mary Penelope Hamilton (née Colthurst) of Blarney Castle in County Cork. He died in 1983, aged ninety-two and is buried with Mary Penelope (who died in 1975) in the Church of the Resurrection, Blarney, Co. Cork.

Fabienne makes other appearances in the annals from time to time. At some point she became a friend of Lord Alfred Douglas: as well as translating his book of poems, she was present

---

136 If there is any lingering doubt as to the background author, the action opens in "Our home – a small 18th Century chateau in a remote part of Gascony…" with mentions of the "lovely reaches" of the Adour River and the "pale birches and the shimmering poplars of St Marsan". Mont-de-Marsan is a town in the Forêts des Landes. Very reminiscent of the Chateau des Tourettes see above.

137 See Appendix 5. Fabienne was also living in the hamlet of Nutbourne: a short uphill walk on foot to Toupie's house, Marehill Road, in Pulborough.

at his funeral in Hove on 23rd March 45.[138] Also present was Lady Edith Fox-Pitt, Bosie's sister, who had been married to St George Lane Fox-Pitt, late of the Society for Psychical Research and once perhaps one time too well known to Radclyffe Hall.

She also makes a brief appearance in the pages of ballerina Irina Baronova's autobiography, as a friend of Helen May Tennant, the sister of Cecil Tennant, the prominent London theatrical agent and close friend of Laurence Olivier and his then wife, Vivien Leigh.

"Another lady appeared, all excited and exuberant... she then fell on me, smothering me in her embrace and exclaiming "C'est magnifique! I am so happy to meet you. I saw you at the ballets. You are magnifique."

"That's Fabienne Hillyard my best friend" explained Helen,[139] interrupting the lady's effusiveness... As for Fabienne she was "the epitome of French femininity".[140]

Fabienne did not marry again although she did live in London for many years enjoying an apparently active wide and active social life. A god daughter living closely comments:

"She was a romantic figure who always wore black lace and jet. She had a beautiful French accent. When I was a child she told amazing bedtime stories..... she lived in Redcliffe Gardens and I a few streets away. She used to hide small presents in her front garden for me to find on my way to school."[141]

Fabienne Hillyard died in a nursing home, 15/16 Westbourne Villas, in Hove, East Sussex, on 13th January 1980. There was a notice in *The Times*:

"HILLYARD – On January 13th 1980 Fabienne, aged seventy-nine, late of 32 Redcliffe Gardens, SW10, daughter

---

138 He is buried at the Friary Church of St Francis and St Anthony in Crawley, West Sussex.
139 Helen May Tennant was the main beneficiary in Fabienne's will, which is dated 1968.
140 *Irina, Ballet Life and Love*, by Irina Baronova (Penguin Group Australia, 2005).
141 With thanks to Camilla von Massenbach.

of the late M. and Mme Brethous-Lafargue, St Sever, France. Comittal service at St Antony and St George Catholic Church, Duncton, West Sussex, Wednesday February 6th at 11.00 AM. Flowers to W B Ryder and sons, Petworth. Memorial mass at Our Lady of Dolours 264 Fulham Road on Wednesday February 20th 6.30PM."

Photo thanks to Elaine O'Neill.

14

Music

Toupie, along with no few other women of the Victorian and Edwardian generation, was very musically talented and in her time had some renown as a composer. Much of her output seems to have survived on paper, although no recordings have yet been found; had there been any, no doubt the disappearance of the gramophone and the eradication of the 78 rpm record would have swept them into history. In Victorian times, and indeed before, many other women gained considerable status for their musical compositions. Two of the most successful, Adela Maddison (1862–1929) and Liza Lehmann (1862–1918), are best known today as composers of songs for voice and piano, and references to "Liza" and "Adela" in social company with Toupie appear from time to time in the diaries of both Mabel Batten and Una Troubridge. Dame Ethel Smyth (1858–1944), a composer of considerable orchestral material, is perhaps the best known of these women today: she also appears to have been an acquaintance of Mabel Batten also a talented composer as well as a singer. The printed musical scores of many of Mabel's compositions are available from the British Library today and it may well be that Toupie's acquaintance with Mabel Batten sprang directly from a musical connection.

Another possible acquaintance may have been the highly regarded Armande de Polignac[142] (1876–1962), a French composer of considerable standing whose name appears on Natalie Barney's doodling "Le Salon de l'Amazone" directly above "T Lowther". She was the niece of Prince Edmond de Polignac, who was married to the highly musical Winnaretta de Polignac, née Singer. The Liedernet Archive contains a known list of Armande de Polignac's compositions; there are excellent recordings of her music for voice and piano on YouTube.

Musical talent and ability does not seem to have been prominent in other members of either the Lowther or the de Fonblanque families. However, Toupie's paternal grandmother, Emilia Cresotti, is named as an Italian opera singer by some sources. Nothing much about her life has been uncovered, unfortunately, and she may well have been of no particular public prominence. But, as an opera singer, she would have been a woman of no little musical talent, and was most likely the family source of Toupie's undoubtedly fine musical ability.

In an interview with the *Evening Telegraph* in May 1898, after a fencing exhibition, Toupie indicates that she is studying singing in Paris with Madame Rosine Laborde (1824–1907), a renowned teacher of singing to the stage stars of the time.

Mme Laborde, 6 May 1898 from the Newspaper Archive.

At a concert at The Wigmore Hall in London one March (unfortunately the extant press cuttings no longer have the full date), two pieces by Toupie Lowther were performed: "Heure du Soir" and "Rêve Basque". At a matinée concert in January 1913, the reporter Mme

---

142 Marie Armande Mathilde de Polignac, Comtesse de Chabannes-La Palice.

Meyerheim praises her music: "it is scholarly – intensely so... original and modern... melodious and impressive"; the cello Sonata she adds, "requires a Casals to do it credit". Some later compositions include more songs, frequently with words by Fabienne Brethous-Lafargue, as well as the composer's versions of the popular "Les Flots" and "Automne". A string quartet was played at a matinée in the Salle Chopin in Paris by the Andolfi Quartet, for which she achieved an ovation from the audience.[143]

The Lowther family would appear to have been supportive of her music lessons: the family address appears in small ads in more than one newspaper:

"Miss Agnes Meyer who has resumed her lessons: highly recommended by Miss Toupie Lowther and others. Terms from Miss Meyer at 73 Pont Street, London."[144]

Who this musical Agnes Meyer actually was and any future musical success has yet to be uncovered.

An unnamed reporter writes of Toupie's music on 18th January 1928: "it is unusual to mix sports and arts... Toupie Lowther... best fencer now quite quickly achieves excellent music. Music difficult and not derivative, can only be played by expert musicians..."

From the little that has survived of her compositions, and the remark of the reporter – "Music difficult and not derivative..." it would seem to be a fair guess that Toupie had received expert tuition in composition that reflected the musical time and tone of the day.

On Monday, 3rd June 1899 at the Criterion Theatre in London, a very fancy Grand Benefit Performance – in front of royalty and large numbers of all shades of the nobility – was held to benefit The Waifs and Strays Society. The dazzling

---

143 Quotations from Toupie's Press Cuttings book held at The Fencing Museum. Not all the titles of the newspaper reports have survived. With many thanks to Malcolm Fare.
144 inter alia the *Morning Post* 3rd May 1899 and *The Times* Digital Archive.

programme included "Incidental music by Miss Toupie Lowther".

On 30th May 1901 a Matinee charitable performance includes Aimée Lowther as "The Pierrot of the Minute" . Followed by Liza Lehmann's new song cycle "The Daisy Chain".[145]

Other tantalizing glimpses include a mention in her will of an "Organ Prelude", which she asks to be played at her funeral (along with her "Ave Maria").

The British Library holds three published settings of poems to piano accompaniment, in the popular Victorian tradition of drawing-room entertainment for voice and piano: "Ave Maria" (1924), "Hazel Eyes" (1922, with words by Oscar Wilde), and a setting of Tennyson's poem "Break, Break, Break" (1901), which have been out of copyright in the UK since 2015. The Bibliotéque Nationale de France holds many more of her compositions (see Appendix 9).

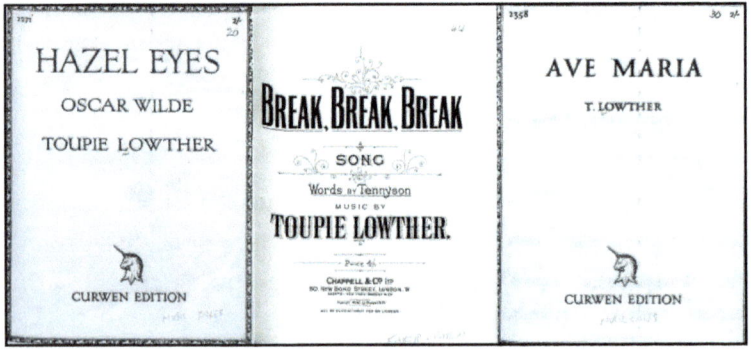

---

145 Liza Lehman was a well known and highly regarded composer of the time. One of her most well known compostions is "In A Persian Garden" 1896.

15

LIFE, DEATH AND HER WILL

For many years Toupie lived in a handsome block of quality flats – 6 Egerton Mansions – in Brompton Road, London. At some time she moved from London to the village of Coldwaltham in West Sussex, acquiring – either renting or buying – a property which she, unsurprisingly, renamed Lowther Cottage. Unfortunately, to this day most of the villagers of "old" Coldwaltham have retained their tradition that all the cottages should be named rather than numbered. So far no identification of a "Lowther Cottage" dating from the 1930s has been located. (The new-build houses that have been plumped towards the far end of the village have followed the more modern numerical system.)

Brief mentions of a house in the French town of Dinard used by Toupie and her siblings, as well as by their mother, appear from time to time in newspapers. Dinard at the time is described as a chic and artistic holiday resort for the wealthy, and it highly possible that the Lowther family either rented or owned a holiday house.

It would seem likely that Toupie's sojourn in Coldwaltham village was a "filling-in period" until her new house, to be named Lowther Lodge, was built in 1934, probably to her own design. It is a fine house on the edge of Pulborough, accessible by a narrow uphill turn off from the main road. Stylish, compact, and handsome, the house overlooks the West Sussex Downs and at the time enjoyed a considerable amount of land. This included a smaller house further up the lane – most likely for a housekeeper and gardener – and, of course, a tennis court. Which remains and is active to this day.

"Lowther Lodge" today, photographed by the writer. The house has a changed name. By kind permission of Mr and Mrs E. D. Thornton.

Miss May "Toupie" Lowther died from "Pulmonary Tuberculosis" on 30th December 1944 at Lowther Lodge, her home in Pulborough, aged almost seventy. The certificate of death indicates that Fabienne D'Avilla was present when she died. Her sister Aimée had also died of tuberculosis nine years before, in 1935 at her home in Brighton: in 1929 Claude Lowther had died at his home in London.

Mary Dexter, a driver in the Hackett Lowther Ambulance Unit, describes Toupie's health in her memoir *In the Soldier's Service, War Experiences of Mary Dexter*.[146] Mary reports that she and Toupie are driving to catch up with the main Hackett Lowther

---

146 Pub. Houghton Mifflin Co. 1918. Available online.

Unit – she drives the GMC and Toupie drives her Wolseley – but their journey is interrupted. Toupie has an "acute attack of intercostal neuralgia" which does not go away, and when they arrive in Paris Toupie is confined to bed from 17th–24th October 1917 with acute pleurisy and a temperature of over 100°F. Mary is professionally interested – "au fond I am a nurse rather than a chauffeuse" – and on 31st October she writes: "Miss Lowther has been very much worse. It was a near thing – and for two days we were all very anxious, but now I am glad to say she is out of danger. They finally took her to the Astoria, the big military hospital in the Champs Elysée nearby. She is the first woman who has ever been a patient there."

On 18 November Mary further writes, "Miss Lowther and Mlle. de M[ontgeon] start south for Arcachon, the lung place on Thursday…and Miss Hackett and I are staying to see them off."

Arcachon is a town in the southwest of France situated, highly favourably for climate, cuisine, and casinos alongside Arcachon Bay, between the Côte d'Argent and the Côte des Landes in Gascony/Aquitaine.[147] During the war large numbers of military hospitals sprang up thereabouts: far away from the battles of Northern France and offering sun, sea and serenity.

"Arcachon – Casino Mauresque de la Ville d'Hiver – 118 beds, reduced to forty in 1919 – Works from 13th February 1915 to 10th July 1915, and as Hospital from 20th July 1915 specializing in non-tuberculous pleural and lung diseases – from January 1919 tuberculosis in particular originating from foreign nationals."[148]

Neither Mary Dexter in her book, nor Lt Chatenay in his diaries make any more concerned references to Toupie's

---

147 The Landes region, near Bordeaux, is where, not too far away, in 1917 a young Fabienne de Brethous-Lafargue is growing up in the Chateau des Tourettes.
148 CHARTE DU FORUM PAGES 14–18: "Hôpitaux militaires dans la guerre 1914–1918 : les principes communes à toute la collection".

health: one has to assume that she recovered well at the time. However, the link between pleurisy and tuberculosis has been long established; lungs already scarred are vulnerable and Toupie was a heavy smoker."

Her will seems to have been put together in much detail, which would indicate that her death did not come quickly. Fabienne D'Avilla and Ralph Stewart Oglethorpe of Petworth, Toupie's solicitor, are named as Executors. Here are some items of value bequeathed to people who have appeared in this narrative, or who are of interest:

"To Madame Gertrude Brethous-Lafargue of Bordeaux my long diamond safety pin."

"To my nephew Claude Barrington[149] my walking sticks, gold Louis XVI match box and any photographs I may have of the late Lieutenant Colonel Claude Lowther my brother… and also all my photographs of the war taken by order of the War Ministry with the instrument used for viewing such photographs."[150]

"To Mademoiselle Gabrielle de Cavelier de Montgeon… my gold ring with the star sapphire, my diamond pig, my little square diamond brooch, my gold sword pin, my snake ring, my empire gold snuff box, and my two diamond eternity rings which belonged to my sister."

"To Mrs Blanche Hillyard my amethyst ring. To Commander George Whiteside Hillyard my new pipes, cigar case, and half a dozen of my occult books."

Her cook, Mrs Manning, gets £500 with a commemoration: "I leave this money in this proportion out of gratitude to Mrs Manning for the attention and many kindnesses she has shown me during the last years of my ill health." Mr. Manning, her husband the gardener, is not left out: he gets £100.

---

149 see Appendix 8.
150 Sadly, whereabouts uknown. Hopefully, one day, they will turn up somewhere.

There are many other bequests of a similar nature, all of which seem to be generous and demonstrate a considerable collection of expensive jewellery. Fabienne is given £4,000 in cash alongside an entreaty for prudence,[151] and £200 is also awarded to Claude Michael John Barrington. The will directs that her remaining estate is to be sold, and a trust fund set up for the benefit of Fabienne D'Avilla during her lifetime: upon Fabienne's death the money is to revert to the trustees and used for the benefit of the Royal Society for the Prevention of Cruelty to Animals, the Anti Vivisection Society, and the British Union for the Abolition of Vivisection.

At her funeral it is Toupie's wish that, along with other music, her composition "Prelude" (for the organ) should be played and her "Ave Maria" sung "by a really good professional soprano or a good choir boy's alto voice, the accompaniment of which can easily be played on the organ, the executants to be given necessary time for rehearsal".

Any references to her funeral, or description of a service, or any local celebration of her life in any way, have not yet been found. Hopefully one day, details of such a commemoration may come to light. The records of Pulborough Parish Church, St Mary's, indicate no burial: a cremation would seem to have been most likely.

Pulborough Parish Church, West Sussex.

---

151 See Chapter 13.

Appendix 1

The Lowther Family

In 1586, William Camden, in *Britannia*, his survey of the British Isles, writes: "Hard by the river Lowther there is a place bearing the same name which hath imparted its name to a family of ancient gentry and worship..."[152]

After centuries of struggle between the Celts and the Saxons, followed by years of invasion and settlement by the Vikings and aggressive visits by the Scottish kings, it was not until 1157 that King Henry II finally and permanently won the wild and bleak counties of the north, Cumberland and Westmorland, for the English crown. The men of the Lowther family make their first recorded appearance in Westmorland at this time: they became knights, made good marriages, and accumulated both land and fortune. They became members of the lower house of parliament, and in the later eighteenth century abandoned the Commons and joined the House of Lords as the Barons Lowther. And then advanced to the earldom of Lonsdale in the early nineteenth century.

The river Lowther still flows its wooded way north from its source at Keld in North Yorkshire, until it joins up

---

152 Ref. *The Lowther Family* by Hugh Owen pub. Phillimore, 1990.

Appendix 1: The Lowther Family

with the Eamont and Eden to empty into the Solway Firth. Whether the river was named for the family or whether the family was named for the river is not known. The Lowther is now a commercial trout fishery and its waters still wander alongside and away from the modern Lowther Park gardens. The park itself is ancient: it was enclosed for hunting by a charter granted by King Edward III in 1337.

The parish church of St Nicholas in the village of Lowther probably dates from about 1170. It was rebuilt around 1686 and much of the original stonework, as well as three Saxon "hogback" tombs, can be identified. St Nicholas is also the parish church for the four other nearby villages of Whale, Hackthorpe, Newtown and Melkinthorp.

"Lowther Hall" in about 1675 extended from the old Pele tower built in the fourteenth century. From The Lowther Family by Hugh Owen.

Exactly when the Lowther family first arrived in this particular quadrant of the north is not recorded. Most likely there would first have been a motte and bailey fortification, which was then upgraded to a more substantial Pele Tower with more comfortable living quarters added later.

Rebuilt again as a red sandstone mansion and renamed Lowther Hall, much of the substantial building was damaged by fire and was eventually taken down, to be replaced with the turreted and towered Lowther Castle, between 1806 and 1814. Lowther Castle however was never fully completed: it was shut up in the 1930s and abandoned to the artistry of the elements.

The castle ruins, the gardens, and the café are open daily 10am to 4pm during the summer.

http://www.lowthercastle.org/

Some of the remains of Lowther Castle in 2015. With thanks to Jay Brady and grundlefly.com.

Appendix 2

The Earl's other children

William 2nd Earl of Lonsdale as an older man. Portrait engraved for the Illustrated London News 1872 from a photograph by Messrs Lewis and Tuck.

William, the second Earl of Lonsdale, did not marry although he did have several natural children. A daughter, Frances Lowther, born in London in 1818, was baptised at St James' Westminster on 29th July 1818; her father is named as "William Lowther". During the previous centuries the name, "Frances", had been frequently given to several daughters of the Lowther family.

Frances Lowther was twenty years older than her half-brother Francis William and seems always to have been happily known as Fanny by her family. Her mother, b. 1791, has been identified as Pierre-Narcisse Champomp – or even Chassepouys – but in later life seems to have been known as Chaspoux. She was a ballerina at The Paris Opera House and came to London in 1815 using the name "Narcisse Gentil", and living in an address then given as 10 Warwick Street.

Sometime later, in London, Narcisse Chaspoux met Dr Charles Lewis Meryon, a physician and surgeon who had been born in Rye in Sussex in 1783. And who was also living at 10 Warwick Street. Narcisse Chaspoux returned to Paris in 1821 taking little Frances with her, and on 23rd November in Paris, presented Charles Lewis Meryon with a son, a half brother for Frances. The baby boy was named as Charles Meryon[153] after his natural father.[154]

Pierre-Narcisse Chaspoux died in Paris in 1838 and little Frances was returned to London to live with her father – at the time styled William, Viscount and Baron Lowther, and serving as an MP in the House of Commons. She lived with him at the Lowther town house, 15 Carlton House Terrace in London: a journey's end which was to be permanent until her marriage in 1840.

Frances Lowther as a young woman. Artist unknown.

Frances Lowther married Henry Broadwood Esquire, a younger son from the well known (and profitable) Broadwood piano manufacturing family. The couple were married on 19th May 1840 at the church of St Martin in the Fields, Westminster in London: the bride receiving a fine dowry of £10,000 from her father. Henry Broadwood did not go into the family business, preferring a political career he became the Member of Parliament for Bridgewater[155] – although one who, during his tenure, would seemingly come to make little impact upon the affairs of the nation.

---

153 *Charles Meryon, A Life* by Roger Collins pub. Garton & Co, Devises 1999.
154 Blog: " L'ŒIL DES CHATS" l'histoire du médecin et de la danseuse le voyage de meryon #2. In French.
155 Now Bridgwater and West Somerset.

Appendix 2: The Earl's Other Children

Frances Broadwood received the benefit of income from a large Trust Fund which was set up for her in her father's will. There is an interesting stipulation: the income from the Trust Fund is for her "sole and separate use independently and exclusively of her husband... or any other husband that she might later take."

There were two sons of the marriage, Arthur and Alfred Broadwood. Both had successful careers in the army: both achieved high rank, both married, and have descendants living. A daughter, Mary Wilhelmina, b. 1851 died as a child aged twelve in 1866. The family lived in Tunbridge Wells in Kent during their marriage: Frances Broadwood died in 1890.

Frances and Henry Broadwood with their young daughter are buried in the churchyard of St Paul, Rusthall near Tunbridge Wells. The grave is placed in the churchyard behind the wall of the apse: there are chains surrounding the stone with a statue representing Faith on a pedestal.

Photograph by the writer

Other natural daughters of William Lowther, are recorded. Marie-Caroline – possibly styled as Lowther, possibly not – was a daughter born to a Caroline Saintfal on 2nd May 1818, and baptised on 4th February 1819 at St George's Anglican church in Paris. No more of her life seems to be known at this time.[156]

A surviving letter from a Mlle Noblet, a dancer at the London opera in 1821, currently lodged in the Cumbria record office indicates that she too bore William Lowther a daughter but also no more is known for certain.[157]

However this Mlle Noblet may well be a Marie-Élisabeth

---

156 Records of St George's Anglican Church in Paris available online.
157 [D/Lons/L1/2/25].

Noblet – known as Lise Noblet, 1801–1852. There is a short Wikipedia page – both the lady's dates of birth and death as well as her occupation as ballerina in the Opera would seem to fit comfortably together.[158]

---

[158] http://en.wikipedia.org/wiki/Lise_Noblet.

Appendix 3

AIMÉE LOWTHER'S WILL

Aimée Lowther died on the 4th February 1935 in her sixty-sixth year and at her house, 10 Montpelier Crescent, Brighton. In her lifetime she composed several wills, more than one has survived, and all demonstrate considerable variations as to beneficiaries. They are extensive, precise and minutely meticulous: littered with codicils and stuffed with bequests and directions. The final codicil is dated 30th January 1935.

Other than a few newspaper reviews, her will[159] is all that positively remains to describe her life and present a portrait of her personality. It may be seen as eccentric today, but when looked at closely displays no little generosity. Her "residential servants" are warmly remembered and a multitude of friends offered "souvenirs". During her lifetime she seems to have accumulated a multitude of antique and artistic collections as well as musical and literary pieces. Her possessions supply a profile to her personality, and her bequests indicate a wide interest in many charitable activities – including the welfare of animals.

The reader becomes very aware that her house in Montpelier Crescent must have been, to say the least, very

---

159 More than one will has survived. A final codicil is dated 30th January 1935.

full[160] of items, preciously collected over no few years and a survey of those valuable items will have to suffice for a glimpse of her character. Her handwriting is individual, large lettered, and prone to being illegible. From these traits alone, the reader could posit that in her time she would have been gently described as strong willed, firm of purpose, and little perturbed by the judgment of her peers. Today, perhaps more severely, as mildly eccentric.

In a previous will of 1930 she bequeaths her house to Claude Michael John Barrington. However, in a rather savage codicil of 1931 the house is removed from her nephew – together with the income from a property in the Isle of Wight – and left in trust for Toupie for her lifetime. A later instruction is that following her death and subsequent sale of the house, the net proceeds are to go to the Battersea Vivisection Hospital "to enable a bed to be founded and maintained and to be known as the Aimée Lowther bed".

Aimée particularly valued a seventeenth-century Topas [sic] Spanish Cross with carbuncle, and an early silver Georgian chocolate pot, a silver-gilt jewelled drinking cup, as well as an oil painting of "The Singing Cherub" attributed to Van Dyke. Also a portrait of her mother, "Mrs Francis Lowther" by Ellen Montalba:[161] sadly whereabouts currently unknown. In her will the portrait was bequeathed to Colonel Alec McBarnet, a cousin on her mother's side. As well as "the walnut Queen Anne writing bureau and… the small watercolour picture of Mother and myself".

Toupie is a major beneficiary as well as an executor (along with the solicitor) and becomes, inter alia, the inheritor of the contents of all the cupboards, bookcases, chests of drawers, etc. in 10 Montpelier Crescent and a set of lapis-handled

---

160 Not to say "brimming".
161 *A Gallery of her Own: An Annotated Bibliography of Women in Victorian Painting*, Elree I. Harris and Shirley R. Scott, pub. Taylor & Francis 2013.

Appendix 3: Aimée Lowther's Will

dinner knives, a crested plated tea tray and all Aimée's pewter articles and a first choice of books and linen – as well as a marble statue of a child on Marine base (in store at Arding & Hobbs Store in Clapham, London) ascribed to Bouchardon. And, interestingly, "all my literary works[162] in a large leather portfolio and in a bound manuscript covered with silk together with papers, photographs, portfolios..."

She also becomes the happy owner of the iron gates which once, probably grandly, fronted Claude Lowther's house in Catherine Street in London, as well as an iron candelabra from Herstmonceux Castle.

Hugh, the 5th Earl of Lonsdale, received a tumbler engraved with the Lowther crest surmounted by a coronet, known as "the Luck of Lowther"; Gabrielle Enthoven, the theatre historian, chronicler, producer and playwright, received a copy of G. F. Watts portrait of Ellen Terry. Another cousin, Captain Philip de Fonblanque, is given a white jade cup and saucer and a crayon picture of "Mrs Francis Lowther", and "an oval crayon picture of Mother and myself". Toupie's goddaughter Fabienne D'Avilla was also remembered, receiving a turquoise blue china set.

She also directs that "the marble statue of the Weeping Child which belonged to [her] late brother Col. Claude Lowther shall be placed on a bracket over his memorial tablet in Hurstmonceux [sic] church, Sussex". Sadly, the marble statue was either not put in place – or, has since, rather unsurprisingly, vanished.

Many of the charities named in Aimée Lowther's will are in business today, indicating that she had some idea that the money would go to a good and expert association. Her legacies also show a wide concern for animal welfare. It is impossible to name them all here, but a selection would seem

---

162 If her own, one presumes unpublished, or possibly the reference is to a book collection.

to demonstrate her personality and final generosity (although her will frequently names the charities with a rather vague accuracy):

- "The Charterhouse Charity for Gentlemen" is now known as "The Charterhouse" and is active today providing accommodation, including some almshouses, for a residential community of single men over sixty years of age.
- "Miss Smallwood's Charity", formed in 1886, received gifts of clothing, linen, shoes and personal articles of apparel; furs; rugs; pillows, blankets and curtains. Now known as "The Society for the Assistance of Ladies in Reduced Circumstances". Her Majesty The Queen honoured the Society by becoming its Patron in 1952.
- "The Distressed Gentlefolk's Aid Association" was founded by Elizabeth Finn in 1897 when she was seventy-two years of age. The charity is now known as "Elizabeth Finn Care" and is active today.
- "The Society of the Holy Child Jesus" received "a rose diamond cross, with carbuncle in the centre and enamel back". It was then and still is now an international community of religious women associated with Catholic schools for girls. The society was founded in England in 1846 by Mother Cornelia Connelly and now has a network of schools spread across its three provinces: Europe, Africa and America.
- "The Sisters of the Poor (St Josephs) Brighton" [*sic*] received all the furniture contained in the two top bedrooms at No. 10 Montpelier Crescent. Now a worldwide charity devoted to the care of the elderly poor, the convent was originally founded in France around 1849 (possibly earlier) by Jeanne Jugan. The convent, presumably also a care home, was in Hove, not Brighton,

at 182 Shoreham Road. Nowadays the Sisters have long left and the site is now a busy industrial complex, but the main access road has, rather nicely, successfully retained the name "St Joseph's Close". Thirteen of the sisters are buried in the Roman Catholic section of Hove cemetery, they have a fine memorial stone.

- One of the many beneficiaries of legacies for the benefit of animals is the "Societé Protectrice des Animaux in Marseilles." The societé is still in existence as "SPA – Marseilles Provence". It cares for and rehomes lost and abandoned animals, has a missing and found list, and is very much still active in animal welfare. Donations are always appreciated. The Societé was founded in 1912.

The names of many others will be familiar: The Home of Rest for Horses; The Metropolitan Drinking Fountain and Cattle Trough Association; Our Dumb Friends League; The Royal Society for the Prevention of Cruelty to Animals. The Animal Defence and Anti-vivisection Society (treasurer the Duchess of Hamilton) is included, and Aimée directs "that such a legacy is conditional on the same being invested and the income there from utilised in human work in defence of horses and beasts of burden in foreign countries according to where the same shall be most needed". After the death of the duchess and some long drawn-out legalities, since 1971 "The Animal Defence Trust" now continues the same work.

Appendix 4

LES RUCHES

"Les Ruches"[163] along with the powerful and charismatic character of the head teacher Mlle Marie Souvestre and her partnership – either personal and/or professional – with Mlle Caroline Dussaut, have passed into an historic cloud of a piquant but permanently attractive drama. Which has, most likely, leapt directly from the fiction of one of their pupils – and later teacher, Dorothy Strachey[164] – and the contents of her solitary but highly successful novel *Olivia*.[165]

Olivia mercilessly describes the passion of a boarding-school girl for her head teacher – who may, or may not, have offered encouragement. The book was instantly popular. In 1951 a film, directed by Jacqueline Audrey and starring Edwige Feuillère as the Headmistress was made in France and rather unpleasantly renamed *The Pit of Loneliness*.

However the plot of *Olivia* the book and *Olivia* aka *The Pit of Loneliness* the film, both bear a much more significant similarity to an original German play of 1930: *Mädchen in*

---

163 See Chapter 5.
164 Later Dorothy Bussy 1865–1960. Her mother Lady Strachey had been a friend of Marie Souvestre: both Dorothy and her sister Elinor attended Les Ruches.
165 Pub. Hogarth Press 1949.

Uniform by the writer Christa Winsloe. Set in a stern, and loveless boarding school for girls in post-war Prussia, a film was swiftly made in 1931. Directed by Leontine Sagan with the screenplay by Christa Winsloe herself, the film retains considerable popularity to this day. However it has also been said that the film was essentially an oblique condemnation of the harsh and loveless Prussian way of life that was inflicted upon the children of the time.

"Natalie Barney and her sister Laura as young women, from Portrait of a Seductress – The World of Natalie Barney *by Jean Chalon. Translated from the French by Carol Barko (Crown Publishers, NY, 1976). Photographer unknown.*

It would be unfair to Toupie to try to paste her into the narrative of *Olivia*, and equally unfair to Natalie and Laura Barney, who were also sent to school at Les Ruches. Daisy White's diary[166] also includes mention of a young Natalie Clifford Barney (1876–1972), later to be celebrated as the "Amazon of Letters", and her even younger sister Laura – who became a talented artist. Both are briefly mentioned by Daisy White, placed amongst the "little ones."

However, were they actually contemporary or not contemporary,[167] then as now, mutual times spent at the same boarding school frequently produce a lifetime's friendship. Much later, Una Troubridge certainly indicates in her diaries that Toupie was well known to Natalie Barney – but rather regretfully for the reader, she seems to have been not at all interested in how and when they first became acquainted.

The mighty American family Roosevelt, which would later produce two presidents and a president's wife, also

---

166 See Chapter 5 "Schooling" *Daisy in Exile: The Diary of an Australian Schoolgirl in France 1887–1889*. Ref: National Library of Australia Canberra 2003.
167 Toupie was two years older than Natalie.

delivered a brace of its daughters into Marie Souvestre's care. "Bamie" (Anna) Roosevelt, Theodore's sister (b. 1855) managed to get to Les Ruches in Avon in France, but her niece Eleanor Roosevelt (b. 1884), future wife of Franklin Delano, missed Les Ruches and Avon, but did get to Marie Souvestre's Allenswood, in Wimbledon Park South London.[168] The story goes that Eleanor did not wish to return home.[169]

Other notable women known to Toupie in the years to come, both socially and in the sporting arena, are said to have been pupils at Les Ruches. They include not only Natalie Barney and her sister Laura, but also Elena Văcărescu, Winaretta Singer – Princess de Polignac, and Olga Maria Beatrice Alberta Caracciolo – Baroness de Meyer. No doubt there were many more.

At this time of writing, the London Borough of Wandsworth maintains that it holds no records of Allenswood School.

---

168 The exact dates for their times in the care of Mlle Souvestre, in either France or England, are not quite clear – but were most likely from about 1899 to 1902.
169 Allenswood, after some changes, continued as a school until 1945.

Appendix 5

Fencing, Fiction, and some Friends

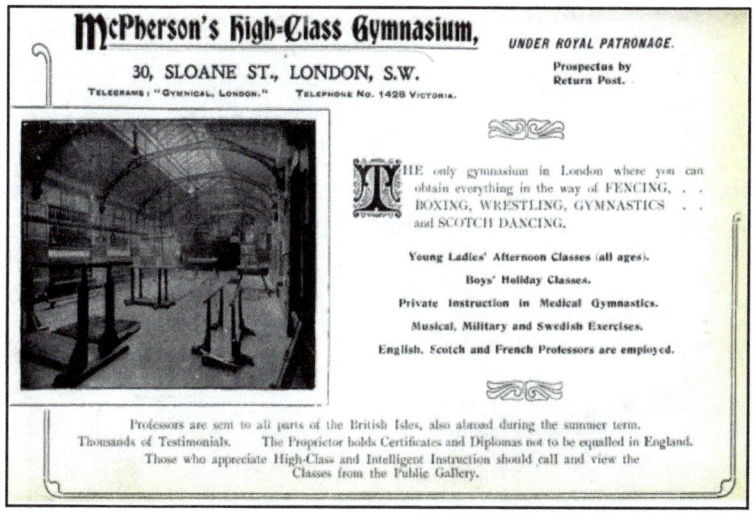

MacPherson's Gymnasium, where Toupie was first taught to fence, also offered many varieties of physical training to ladies of all ages. Classes were not mixed; women's gymnastics took place on Thursday evenings, whilst "special afternoon classes" were held every Tuesday and Friday.[170]

The address of 30 Sloane street is within easy distance of 73 Pont Street SW, the home of Captain Francis William Lowther

---

170 Publicity for MacPherson's with thanks to Tony Wolf.

and his family. McPherson's Gym also offered training in the art of "Bartitsu" – a new defensive martial art that was all the rage in London around 1900 when a mugging and thugging were very real threats to well-dressed gentlemen out for the evening.[171] Bartitsu classes were very much sought after and, in theory anyway, were fully open to women (unusually at this time). Bartitsu included the use of the fist in offensive manoevres, and it would have been well within her character that Toupie tried her hand at a martial art that would utilise the swift strong arm and the neatly dancing footwork of the experienced and highly competent fencer. Possibly the not-infrequent nudge that Toupie also practised boxing stems from the odd sparring practice at McPherson's.

Historically, Bartitsu is said to have been practised by "Mrs Pankhurst's Bodyguard" formed from a few chosen women, all carefully selected from the more belligerent ranks of the Women's Social and Political Union.[172] The Pankhurst Bodyguards appear *en masse* in an adventurous graphic novella – as does Toupie in a small but singular role as Mrs

From Blood and Honor, *"The Foreworld Graphic Novels Saga, – Suffrajitsu – Mrs. Pankhurst's Amazons" by Tony Wolf and Joao Viera, copyright 2015 by Foreworld, LLC., USA. Toupie is driving Mrs Pankhurst.*

---

171 Edward Barton Wright, *Jujitsu and Judo: the Japanese Art of Self Defence from a British Athletic Point of View*, February 1901.
172 Their trainer and leader was Mrs Edith Garrud (1872–1971).

Appendix 5: Fencing, Fiction, And Some Friends

From Suffrajitsu: Mrs Pankhurst's Amazons: *the ladies have been loaded into a soft top lorry. Toupie is in the sports jacket seated at the front on the right.*

Pankhurst's driver/chauffeuse – and who is also, with others, at the moment of high drama, captured by the enemy.

Other Fencers

Toupie Lowther was by no means the only celebrated woman fencer of her time. No few well-born and leisured women of Europe and America also fiercely embraced the Salle d'Armes, the mask and the foil. One of the prominent European women fencers of Toupie's generation was Olga de Meyer (1871–1930).

She was born Maria Beatrice Olga Alberta Caracciolo in London in 1871, a daughter of the son of a Neapolitan nobleman – the Duke of Castellucio – and his wife.[173] In 1892 she married first a nobleman from Naples, and then the photographer Adolphe de Meyer, who would come to build himself a successful worldwide career as a photographer.[174]

---

173 She is also rumoured to have been a daughter of the Prince of Wales, later King Edward VIII.
174 Later styled "Baron de Meyer".

The marriage – which is quoted as being "lavender" – seems to have been very successful and lasted over thirty years, propelling the couple into the international London-based jet-set of their time. Newspaper cuttings indicate that Olga de Meyer began to fence in Paris[175] in 1902 under Prof Boulége.

Later in 1909 she represented Salle Mimiague in London for the first ladies' team competition in December 1909. With her team-mates Mrs Edwards (Capt.), Toupie Lowther, and a Miss Earp, they came second to the winning team from the Salle Bertrand. This seems to have been the last time that Toupie fenced in public competition.

"This exceedingly able and withal particularly graceful fencer, the Baroness de Meyer, is a pupil of Mimiague of The Sword Club. Both last year and the year before she fought her way into the final pool of the Ladies' Amateur Championship, a proof that she stands quite in the front rank of fencers. She relies for her success at the art mainly by defence, with a strong rally mainly of sixte and [sic] riposte."[176]

Olga de Meyer. Original photographer unknown.

Olga de Meyer was closely associated with Winaretta, Princess de Polignac née Singer:[177] a highly accomplished musician who supported many women composers including Ethel Smyth and Adela Maddison Both ladies are signed in as guests on Natalie Barney's "Salon de l'Amazone",[178] as is Colette.

Winnaretta de Polignac is said to have paid, or otherwise cajoled, the artist

---

175 *Les Armes*, magazine, probably 1909.
176 The information about Baroness Olga de Meyer and the image has been kindly provided by Malcolm Fare from the National Fencing Museum.
177 *Music's Modern Muse – A Life of Winnaretta Singer, Princesse de Polignac* by Sylva Kahan (University of Rochester Press, 2003).
178 See Appendix 11.

Appendix 5: Fencing, Fiction, And Some Friends

Romaine Brooks[179] to paint her portrait. Sadly, neither the whereabouts, nor possibly the fate, of the portrait is known. A photograph from an unspecified early-twentieth-century exhibition catalogue is said to be in the possession of the Singer family.

The Singer-Polignac Foundation is still independently active in the pursuit and patronage of the arts, musical excellence and human and medical sciences. It was initially set up in 1928 by a generous grant from the princess de Polignac, and is situated in Paris.

Winaretta de Polignac and Colette, the French writer and novelist both in later life. Original photographer unknown.

As yet there is no easily located connection between Olga de Meyer, Winaretta de Polignac, Colette and Toupie, yet the overlap of the years between them, the close friendship of Natalie Barney, as well as the overwhelming tide of sport and music which filled so much of both their lives, makes a lack of acquaintance a matter that cannot be seriously considered.

---

179 For more information about Romaine Brooks and Natalie Barney see *Between Me and Life* by Meryle Secreste pub. Macdonald & James, London, 1976.

Appendix 6

The Hillyard Family

Commander George Whiteside Hillyard (1864–1943) and his wife, Blanche, née Bingley, (1863–1946) were friends of Toupie's of some considerably long standing. They knew her from far-off days in and around the early British and European-wide tennis championships, followed after (semi) retirement with weekend sporting visits to The Elms at the village of Thorpe Satchville – their one-time country home in Leicestershire.

George Hillyard was a naval man for eight years, progressing from young cadet to midshipman and then to sub-lieutenant. As a midshipman he served on HMS Bacchante for two years, alongside the Princes Albert Victor and George,[180] two of the grandsons of HM Queen Victoria. This may well be the origin of the coveted royal association with the All England Tennis Championships at Wimbledon, which continues to this day.

George Hillyard left the Navy aged twenty-one. Always a betting man, he then embarked on a sporting career as a top-rank cricketer and tennis player, a swimmer and an oarsman. Name the sport and he excelled. He was Secretary of the All

---

180 Who would later become King George V.

Appendix 6: The Hillyard Family

England Lawn Tennis Club from 1907 to 1924 and during the Great War, working in London, he returned to naval service in a position that he later declined to talk about. He rose to the rank of Commander.

Blanche Bingley was born in Greenford, Middlesex, the daughter of a wealthy family. Early on she became a member of the Ealing Lawn Tennis Club and played her first ever Wimbledon Ladies' Championship in 1884: thus beginning a formidable string of appearances in the All England Ladies Championships. A quote from the online Tennis Forum says it all: "Blanche Hillyard appeared in a record thirteen ladies' singles final at Wimbledon, winning the title six times, in 1886, 1889, 1894, 1897, 1899 and 1900, and being runner-up in 1885, 1887, 1888, 1891, 1892, 1893 and 1901."[181]

They married in July 1887 and in the course of time had two children: a son, Jack Montagu, and a daughter, Marjorie Anastasie, both born at The Elms.

Well known to all the tennis players of the time, the Hillyards' house and home was always referred to simply as Thorpe Satchville. They were generous with their hospitality, regularly welcoming and entertaining all manner of tennis and golf and any other sporty players – and their friends – to their house parties. Entertainment involved "in-house" tennis matches (with serious wagering on the results), and expeditions to local tennis tournaments were very frequent. Blanche Hillyard was also a breeder of beagles, and hunting on foot was also a popular pastime.

Unsurprisingly "Thorpe Satchville" – its hospitality, house parties, sporting entertainment and all round fun – including no few bets and wagers – became known to its visitors as an "Institution" rather than just a house.

---

181 With thanks to the gentlemen of The Tennis Forum http://www.tennisforum.com/.

Commander, Mrs and J. M. Hillyard, from photo from Forty Years of First Class Lawn Tennis *pub. Williams & Norgate Ltd, 1924.*

Toupie was a regular visitor and player, and Mabel Batten's diary includes a description of a visit with her to the Hillyards. However, time and life speeds by, and in 1926, after thirty years of serious work and weighty play at Thorpe Satchville, all the Hillyards left Leicestershire and moved south, to West Sussex, taking up residence in a fine property, Bramfold House, in Nutbourne, a village very close to Pulborough. A considerable spread of land was attached, and, as would be expected, tennis courts and a golf course were soon installed.

As a golf player George Hillyard became a co-founder of the prestigious West Sussex Golf Club, which opened its fine course and handsome clubhouse in 1929. The club remembers Commander George Hillyard as a player and a gentleman: he donated a handsome silver trophy which is still on display at the clubhouse.

George Hillyard died in 1943 aged seventy-nine. After his death Blanche moved with her daughter Marjorie to a smaller house in Batts Lane, Pulborough, which was named Greenford. The house is only a few minutes' walk along the lane and up the hill to Toupie's house, "Lowther Lodge" in Mare Hill Road. Blanche Hillyard died in 1946 aged eighty-three.

Jack Hillyard, although married twice, had no children from either marriage. He died in 1983 at Blarney Castle, County Cork in Ireland. Marjorie Hillyard, his sister, was disabled and did not marry. She lived until 1956.

Appendix 6: The Hillyard Family

George and Blanche Hillyard lie together in the churchyard of St Mary's Church Pulborough. There are no known descendants.

Appendix 7

THE GERMAN SPRING OFFENSIVE OF 1918 AND MORE ABOUT THE HACKETT LOWTHER AMBULANCE UNIT

The Russo-Franco Treaty of Alliance of 1892 had bound Russia to support France, should French territory ever be threatened by any armed invasion. As a result, in 1914, when Germany invaded France – in the west[182] – German armies also invaded Russia – in the east.[183] A second front line, The Eastern Front, was then established between Germany and Russia.

However, in March 1918, when the kingdom of Rumania had joined the war with the Western Allies and the kingdom of Bulgaria followed suit alongside the Central Powers, the new Bolshevik revolutionary government in Russia swiftly signed a peace treaty with Germany. The treaty is known, historically, as the Treaty of Brest-Litovsk.[184]

With the fighting on the Russian Eastern Front over, the German divisions that had been serving there made their way back to Germany to prepare to head west for France. For the

---
182 The Battle of Mons, August 1914.
183 The Battle of Tannenberg, August 1914.
184 After the war had come to an end in November 1918, the Treaty of Brest-Litovsk was terminated.

Appendix 7: The German Spring Offensive of 1918

Western Allies it was not a question of whether a reinforced German invasion would come west but when! By April 1918 the mighty German Spring Offensive of 1918 was heading into France.

The Offensive of 1918[185] comprised a series of "advances": "Michael" was launched on 21st March 1918, "Georgette" on 9th April, "Blücher-Yorck" on 27th May and "Gneisenau" on 9th June.[186] Michael, Georgette and Blücher-Yorck began the advance successfully, pushing back the Allied armies some 20km in many places, but gradually began to run out of energy and ground to a halt. Gneisenau was launched against the French sector and was also initially successful, but on 11th June four divisions of the French Tenth Army, under General Mangin, struck back. They first halted and then grimly began to push the German forces back across the destroyed and devastated ground that they had come.

The Hackett Lowther Ambulance Unit served as members of the French army during the days of the Gneisenau German Army advance – and then its retreat. Working through the day and then into the night and then again into the day, the women drove to and picked up the wounded, returning to the train station at Creil, and then back again. Without headlamps, along broken and bombed and shell torn roads, not infrequently under fire, bomb, and gas attack.

The 100-day Allied Offensive – the long-sought retaliation – had been launched on 8th August 1918, and by 5th October the Allies had successfully fought back and broken through the entire depth of the German defences. On the 11th day of the 11th month of 1918, at 5am, an Armistice agreement with

---
185 "Kaiserschlacht": also known as Ludendorff Offensive.
186 Gneisenau is also known as The Noyon-Montdidier Offensive and The Battle of Metz.

the Allies was signed by a German delegation in a railway carriage outside the town of Compiègne, to come into effect later that day, at 11am, Paris time. The war on the Western Front had ground to a permanent halt.[187]

More about WWI and the Hackett Lowther Unit

All soldiers carried their own first aid kit to mop up minor wounds. However if the soldier was clearly in need of urgent hospital treatment, he would be temporarily patched up at a "First Aid Post" – also known as a "Field Ambulance Unit/ Poste de Secours" and/or an "Advanced Dressing Station". From there an ambulance[188] would deliver him smartly to a nearby "casualty clearing hospital"[189] given immediate nursing and treatment and then being sent on to a base hospital. Or perhaps to a train station to an ambulance train where he would also be professionally nursed and treated during the journey to the base hospital. Well away behind the battle lines. He would then be further treated, hopefully recover, and then be sent back to the front. Or, with any luck, his journey would continue on to yet another a hospital this time back home in in Blighty.[190]

---

187 This short description of the German Spring offensive Gneisenau Advance is by no means detailed and is meant only as a backdrop. There are many books available on the complexity of the German Spring Offensive of 1918, not to mention the Internet.
188 In some areas horse-drawn ambulances continued to be used throughout the war.
189 Royaumont, the Scottish Women's Hospital in France, was a Casualty Clearing Hospital. See *The Women of Royaumont* by Eileen Crofton pub. Tuckwell Press 1997.
190 Creil Railways Station was a stopping point for WWI Ambulance/ Hospital trains. The Ambulance trains had carriages modified into mobile hospital wards and trained and maintained their own individual railway nurses.

Appendix 7: The German Spring Offensive of 1918

Recruitment

How Toupie located, collected, and signed up her drivers for service can only be guessed at: many must have been previous friends and acquaintances, and others located by word of mouth in and around other ambulance units or by encouraging advertisment. In her Report held at the Imperial War Museum, she indicates that Frances Donisthorpe – who had served in Serbia as second-in-command of a Scottish Women's Hospitals ambulance unit – gave "invaluable assistance".

Publicity however, was not to be excluded. The *Evening Standard* reporter "Corisande", in his chatty and timely column "Woman's World and its Ways". Lavish in his praise he has a piece headlined:

DRIVING AMBULANCES IN FRANCE.

I "Miss Toupie Lowther... a first class tennis player and a champion fencer... who wants women with experience as motorcar drivers and capable of doing their own running repairs, to volunteer as drivers in the Hackett Lowther Ambulance Unit attached to a division of the French Army."

As well as Miss Lowther "being glad to see applicants at 6 Egerton Mansions, Brompton Road,"[191] he adds "alternatively they can apply at the Women's Legion Headquarters, 116 Victoria Street, SW".[192]

Badge of the Women's Legion.

The Women's Legion was formed in 1915 to recruit young women workers into jobs about to be left vacant by the anticipated grip of the 1915 National Registration Act and the

---

191 Toupie's home for many years. The building is still there but unfortunately the numbers of the flats have been much altered. See Chapter 1.
192 *Evening Standard*, date unknown but probably 1917.

1916 and 1918 Military Service Acts, either by "dilution" or "substitution". The legion was very successful and by 1918 was also operating in partnership with the newly formed "Women's Corps", known as the Women's Army Auxiliary Corps. The Motor Transport Section of the Women's Legion, although providing drivers for work both at home and in France, was clearly still open to other recruitments.

The Hackett Lowther Uniform and a few others.

Toupie's tunic with her galons on the left arm and war medal ribbons attached. After the war she donated her uniform to the IWM where it survives.
With thanks to the IWM.

The uniform of the Unit, as well as the tunic, blouse and tie, included a smart cap and a wide skirt falling just above the ankle. By no means what we would consider to be ideal nowadays when its wearer often had to scramble in and out of heavy motor vehicles, change wheels and tyres, lift and prop up cumbersome engine bonnets as well as helping and hauling up the wounded into the ambulance. Some women – the Hector Munro Unit for example – did wear breeches covered up under a knee length tunic with gaiters handsomely laced up to the knee. [193] Some of the women who served with the Hackett Lowther Ambulance Unit wrote of their experiences later, and a few photographs have survived.

---

193 Which became a uniform handsomely re-invented as ideal gardening gear by Vita Sackville-West some years later.

Appendix 7: The German Spring Offensive of 1918

The Film

Katherine Hodges in her narrative describing her service during the war, describes how a short film of the Unit was made at the Château Le Fayel on 8th July 1918. The film has now been digitised and is available at the French Photographic Archives: the reference is 14-18 A 853.

Mary Dexter

Mary Dexter was an American volunteer who, from 1914–1915, had spent the first few months of the war as a probationer nurse at the American Women's War Relief Hospital in Devon. She then nursed at hospitals in Belgium and France, returning to London to train at The Medico-Psychological Clinic for the "Treatment of Nervous Disabilities – symptoms of what was then known as "War Shock".

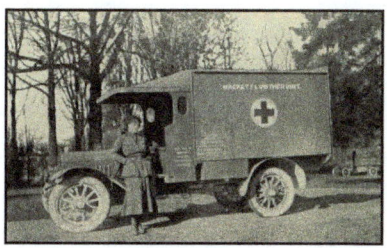

Mary Dexter photographed beside her own ambulance. Photographer unknown.

She came from a wealthy family, and either from her own money or from the wealth of her family donated her own ambulance, a GMC.[194] Mary Dexter did her bit: but she left the unit in May 1918 after injuring her back when cranking her GMC,

---

194 Short for General Motors Company: *inter alia* military vehicles, trucks and vans.

and so did not go to Wiesbaden after the war. She married Guy Napier-Martin (b. 1883 in London) in 1919. Their first and third children survived infancy: a boy and a girl.[195]

In the pages of *In the Soldier's Service* Mary Dexter gives a close-up view of The Hacket-Lowther Unit (Motor Section) – the cumbersome and unpredictable canvas-topped vehicles, the weighty tyres and unreliable carburettors, alongside the joy of a hot cup of cocoa. She also writes of a conversation with Toupie in 1917 in which "Miss Lowther says it took five months once for some tooth powder to reach her!" This would seem to confirm that Toupie had spent some considerable time in France, during the war, before the Unit was set up.

Katherine Hodges

Toupie and Miss Hodges with thanks to Paul Handford.

Katherine Hodges (1888–1982) was a daughter of the playwright Horace Hodges, and had served in the Scottish Women's Hospitals as a driver on the Eastern Front. On the collapse of Russia and the Revolution, she, with others, escaped back to England. She was awarded the Russian medal of St George and the Order of St Stanislaus. In 1917 she joined the Hackett Lowther Unit as a driver and in France and was awarded the Croix-de-Guerre.

Katherine Hodges wrote home on 28th August 1918: "At Pimprez the night before last we were gas shelled all night, had to wear our gas masks for five hours. Perfectly awful, you feel you can't breathe in the beastly things. I was standing talking

---

195 *In the Soldier's Service War Experiences of Mary Dexter 1914–1918* pub. Houghton Mifflin Company, October 1918.

Appendix 7: The German Spring Offensive of 1918

in the evening to a soldier in front of my car and the nightly hymn of hate (the German shelling and bombing) at the other end of the village when suddenly Whizz Crash and a 210 (very large shell) burst about six hundred yards away in an orchard. There was a perfect shower of fragments of shell, and a bit the size of a nut hit my shoulder, but only bruised it. I retired to the dug-out quickly, accompanied by my soldier friend. They plunked them over for about two hours. Fortunately there were no wounded to be taken at the moment so one could stay in the dug-out. They are very good about not sending you out under bombardment unless it is very pressing."[196]

At the end of the war Katherine Hodges did not go to Germany with the Unit. She married an army officer, Peter North, seemingly there were no children of the marriage. In the Second World War she stepped into uniform again and put herself back behind the wheel as an ambulance driver in war-torn London. After this war she retired to Sussex.

Barbara Stirling

Barbara Edith Stirling (1891–1966) was born in London: her family home was in Goring-on-Thames (then in Oxfordshire.) At the beginning of the war she trained as a VAD, worked as a nurse, then joined up with the Serbian Relief Fund[197] as a driver. In 1916, taking her Ford car with her, she went by ship

---

196 Quoted from Katherine Hodges "Memorial – An account of her experiences in WWI".
197 The Serbian Relief Fund was based in London. The committee organised fully staffed and equipped volunteer Hospital "Units" which were sent out to Serbia. The committee was mainly made up of women.

to Salonika[198] and seems to have arrived after the successful Monastir[199] Allied offensive against Bulgaria. Barbara returned home in 1917, signed up with the Hackett Lowther Ambulance Unit, and went straight off to France. She received the Serbian Medal, the Cross of the Serbian Order, and the Croix-de-Guerre.

Lt Victor Henri Léon Chatenay

Victor Chatenay (1886–1985) was one of those people who keep a diary. Throughout the war he kept a record of his life and experiences and in 1968 published them, expanded into readable and delightful French. He has left us a description of himself and his time with the Hackett Lowther Unit alongside Toupie and the other women: some of whom particularly caught his attention and are mentioned individually. His diaries provide a full description of the Unit's service during a critical time of the war, as well as some not always flattering analysis of the individual temperament and appearance of some of the drivers.

Serving in the French army from 1914, Lt Chatenay was badly wounded early on in the war, returning to active service as a non-combatant officer. Although at first not at all pleased to be placed with not only an English canteen and ambulance Unit, but also one made up wholly of womenfolk. He staggered, came round, and eventually became rather impressed by the women of the Unit, probably helped by discovering that no few had come from prominent and wealthy families. And as an officer and a gentleman he set himself a stern target to do his absolute and professional best

---

198 There was an (Eastern) Allied Front at Salonika: during the war there was no way to cross Europe by land, the sea journey through the Mediterranean was the only way. Thessalonika is now a Unesco World Heritage site.
199 Now often known as Bitola or Bitolj.

Appendix 7: The German Spring Offensive of 1918

for all of his drivers. He would be totally scrupulous and sternly efficient: professional – even deliberately distant – with the English Mesdames, and to insist on his authority being regarded with full formal military respect at all times.

His job included the responsibility of receiving all orders from his immediate superiors, finding and maintaining the location of potential billets for his drivers and making sure that rations could be accessed promptly. He was responsible for the issue of gas masks and blankets, as well as obtaining adequate supplies of petrol, tools and lamps. And, directing and inspiring the ceaseless paperwork as well as supervising his own staff: the maréchal des logis – who acted as secretary and his personal driver, the auto mechaniques and the cook. And making sure that Miss Lowther managed the day-to-day organisation and discipline of the women drivers.

His narrative provides striking close-up snapshots of the ladies of the Hackett Lowther Unit at work and at play, their whims, foibles, scrapes and adventures. In his published diaries he recounts an episode in late 1918 when the Unit was in Metz. Driver Barbara Stirling, at one of the evening entertainments, just happened to be dancing with the almighty Marshal Pétain.

"I dance very poorly mademoiselle," said he. "Yes, mon general," she replied, "but you have won the War!" Marshal Petain laughed and replied: "That is very nice for you to say so young lady, I shall always remember it." In 1940, Barbie [Barbara] said [to me] "If I had known, I would have stamped on his foot."[200]

And indeed, as was to be expected, with an unmarried and highly respectable young man of just over thirty, daily surrounded by a multitude of (mostly) unmarried, practically-minded and very well-brought-up young women, a romance was inevitable.

---

200 Victor Chatenay, *Mon Journal de Quatorze–Dix-huit* (L'Imprimerie de l'Anjou, 1968).

In 1919 Victor Chatenay, aged thirty-thtree, married Barbara Edith Stirling, aged twenty-eight. The engagement was published in *The Times* of 20th August 1919 and the happy couple were married at the Catholic Church of Our Lady and St John's in Goring-on-Thames, on 1st October 1919. No reports of the marriage in the local papers have been found, possibly because it took place in a Catholic church. Victor Chatenay took his wife back to his home at Angers in France, and in the years to come she presented him with a fine family of four sons and a daughter.

Twenty years after the marriage, war came back to France. Victor Chatenay, became active in the French Resistance and when Angers was occupied by the German army he was arrested and imprisoned for six months by the Gestapo being eventually released. Immediately he was flown to London on a Lysander aircraft supplied by the British Government where he stayed, until the end of the war. Barbara remained in Angers with their youngest son and even younger daughter: continuing to work for the Resistance. She was arrested by the Gestapo in 1944 and sent to Ravensbrück concentration camp in the far east of Germany.

Their first, second, and third sons served in WWII. During the war the third son was killed in France, sadly by friendly fire. The youngest son, still a very young man, also took part in the Resistance: he too was captured by the Gestapo in 1944 and sent to Buchenwald concentration camp. He survived and at the time of writing is still living aged ninety-one.

Barbara Chatenay survived Ravensbrück. She was taken to Sweden on one of the Bernadotte "White Buses"[201] in 1945,

---

[201] In 1945 Folke Bernadotte, a Swedish diplomat and nobleman, using white buses provided by the Swedish Red Cross, rescued many survivors from the German concentration camps before the end of the war. They were taken to Sweden. For information about the women of Ravensbrück, the dreadful deaths, and the so called "liberation" by the Russian army, see *If This is a Woman – Inside Ravensbrück: Hitler's Concentration Camp for Women*, by Sarah Helm (Little, Brown, 2015).

just before the arrival of the of the Red Army. She died in 1966.

Victor Chatenay served three times as Mayor of Angers: he died in 1985 aged ninety-nine. There is a Rue Barbara Stirling in Angers as well as an Avenue Victor Chatenay. They have descendants living.[202]

The marriage of Lt Victor Chatenay to Barbara Stirling at Goring-on-Thames 1919.
Many thanks to Mme Veronique Chatenay-Dolto, a granddaughter of the marriage, and also to Janet Hurst, the local historian from Goring-on-Thames.

---

202 Victor Chatenay: *Mon Journal du Temps du Malheur* (Editions du Courrier de L'Ouest" 1967).

Appendix 8

A Few Other People

Claude Michael John Barrington

Claude Michael John Barrington cropped from an original school cricket group now in the public domain. With thanks to Marlborough College.

Born somewhere around 1895/6, Claude Michael John Barrington is said to have maintained that he was born in Paris, a son of Claude Lowther, which would have made him the nephew of Aimée and Toupie. No original certificate of Claude Barrington's birth has ever been located, although the date of 15th January 1896 appears on at least one easily located legal document, a record of his War Service 1914–1918, held at the British National Archives. Dated August 1918, the document gives 15th January 1896 as his date of birth, alongside his permanent home address as Hurstmonceux Castle, Sussex. The "Person to be Informed of Casualty" is "Col. Claude Lowther, also of Hurstmonceux Castle in Sussex": Relationship "Uncle".

Appendix 8: A Few Other People

Claude Barrington[203] was sent to school at Marlborough College, and appears in a photograph of the then Cricket XI in early 1914. Leaving just before the war broke out, he joined the Durham Light Infantry as a second lieutenant, but later managed a transfer to the Royal Flying Corps (which was later renamed the Royal Air Force). He survived the war and returned to his regiment, retiring in 1928; he remained on the reserve officer list until 1944. He seems not to have had any later permanent profession.

Aimée Lowther must have attended his first wedding in 1918, to Katherine Wardrop, as her signature features on the marriage certificate as a witness. The certificate also, interestingly, records the grooms father's name as "Michael Barrington, deceased". Claude Barrington's first child, a daughter, born in 1919, was named Toupie. She apparently did not take to "Toupie", however, and abandoned the name later in life. Claude Barrington married twice more, and has descendants still living. He died in 1971 and is buried at St Mary's Church in Thame.

In his will Claude Lowther set up individual and, indeed, substantial trust funds for the benefit of not only Claude Barrington but also a Kenneth Cunningham, including a legacy to Dr Armando Child in lieu of fees for the care of Kenneth Cunningham. Little more of Kenneth Cunningham is known, and as yet neither an identifiable birth nor death certificate has been located. At the memorial service for Claude Lowther on Saturday, 30th June 1929, the named members of the congregation included not only his two sisters but also Claude Barrington and Kenneth Cunningham.[204]

Years later, both Aimée and Toupie Lowther, in their own wills, would be openly generous to Claude Barrington, both referring to him as "my nephew". Toupie's will, indeed,

---

203 Barrington was a surname from the de Fonblanque family.
204 *The Sussex Express*, 5th July 1929.

goes further and specifies Claude Barrington "as the son of my brother". This can, however, be interpreted two ways: as either assumed fact, or the maintenance of a long-held fiction.

The Spanish Infanta

The Spanish writer and historian Ricardo Mateos Sáinz de Medrano has published a biography of the Spanish Infanta Eulalia de Borbón y Borbón (1864–1958), the youngest daughter of Queen Isabella II,[205] and married to Antonio de Orléans y Borbón, Duke of Galliera. The author describes how, having given him two sons, the Infanta Eulalia separated from her husband.

Sáinz de Medrano indicates that the Infanta Eulalia may well have been, and very likely was, the birth mother of the child who would come to be named Claude Michael John Barrington and who was brought up in England, East Sussex, by Claude Lowther. His opinion is very balanced, and even more so to the view that the hitherto unknown and blameworthy father of this child may, in fact, have well been the Infanta's known lover, Count George Louis James Mario Eulalio Jamatel.

His book describes that the Infanta's husband believed this to be so; he and his wife had been living apart for two years.

---

205 Queen Isabella II reigned as Queen Regnant of Spain from 1833 to 1868, when she was deposed. In 1874 Eulalia's eldest brother Alfonso was restored to the Spanish throne as Alfonso XII.

Appendix 8: A Few Other People

Sir Henry Drummond Wolff

Claude Lowther arrived in Madrid as a raw and new attaché at the British Embassy in 1894, under the then British Ambassador to Spain, Sir Henry Drummond Wolff GCB, GCMG, PC (1830–1908). Sir Henry and his family had been guests at the marriage of Francis Willian and Louise Beatrice Lowther back in 1868: Sir Henry had "raised the toast" to the bride's father, Edward Barrington de Fonblanque, and Adeline,[206] his daughter had been one of the bridesmaids.

Sir Henry Drummond Wolff, available online. Thanks to the original unknown photographer.

It may well be that it was Sir Henry himself who arranged a silent removal of the Infanta's child to London and into the care of Claude Lowther, his former attaché in Madrid. Providing a neat exit from an unwanted diplomatic career – though not necessarily to the approval of Claude's parents.

It of course remains possible that Claude Lowther may have genuinely been the father. But, strangely, in no document now readily available (such as his will) does he refer to either Claude Barrington, or Kenneth Cunningham for that matter, as a son, adopted or otherwise. Nor does he refer to himself as a guardian or the boys as his wards or in any way, either as relatives or adoptees.

Claude Barrington also makes no appearance as a beneficiary in the respective wills of Francis and Louise Lowther. As the parents of three children, both must have anticipated, indeed yearned, to have grandchildren in their lives. However, what really happened by now can only remain of consequence to the younger generations of the descendants

---

206 Later the writer Lucas Cleeve.

of Claude Barrington. The event, and the very skilled cover-up to protect the Infanta and her child, and thus the credence of the historic Bourbon monarchy of Spain (always swaying on thin ice), took place over a hundred years ago and, no doubt, as was then deliberately intended, will always slide away from solid scrutiny. And so maintain the continuance of a family's privacy.

Echoes however do appear.

The Times Newspaper of 25th January 1899 describes a "Grand Morning Concert, in aid of Charity", to be held at Grosvenor House (by kind permission of the Duke of Westminster!) Inter alia, music was to be by, Clara Butt and Mr Kennerely Rumford – both professional singers – a Mrs Duncombe (from a family no doubt also to have been musically artistic) and W. H Squire a cellist. Other entertainment was no doubt welcome: "Miss Toupie Lowther has also kindly promised to give an Exhibition in Fencing. Tickets (one guinea and a half a guinea) from Miss Rowe, 31 Beauchamp Place.[207] There is to be two ladies of royalty present – HRH Princess Henry of Battenburg and HRH the Infanta Eulalia of Spain."

Sir Henry himself was no stranger to that which cannot be spoken of. His wife, Adeline Douglas, was a daughter of novelist Walter Sholto Douglas and his "wife", Isabella Douglas née Robinson. Walter Sholto Douglas, writing under the name David Lyndsay, was in fact a woman cross dresser, Mary Diana Dods,[208] an illegitimate daughter of a Scottish earl.

As a man accustomed to hidden family secrets and at the time heading towards the fringe of retirement from a very successful career, a participation in the removal of the Infanta's

---

207 Presumably Miss Nellie Rowe, see Chapter 15.
208 *Mary Diana Dods, a Gentleman and a Scholar* by Betty T. Bennett. Pub. William Morrow & co. Inc. NY 1991

Appendix 8: A Few Other People

child into the care of Claude Lowther via the diplomatic bag, is very plausible.

Sir Henry Drummond Wolff retired in 1900, he died at a hotel in Brighton in 1908 aged seventy-seven years. A grassy plaque in Brighton Woodvale Cemetery, placed there in the 1960s, marks his resting place. He has descendants living.[209]

---

209 *Death and the City* by Rose Collis, Pub. 2013 Hanover Press.

Appendix 9

MORE MUSICAL COMPOSITIONS

Many of Toupie's published compositions are held at the Bibliothèque nationale de France filed under "Lowther T.". This list is from the 2015 catalogue although the 2014 catalogue bearsa few differences.

Her music was originally published by Éditions Maurice Senart, a company which operated in Paris from 1908 to 1941. Fabienne Brethous-Lafargue has supplied many of the texts:

"Trois Melodies. Chant et piano": éditions Maurice Senart 1925

"Au Loin". Poésie de F. Brethous-Lafargue: éditions Maurice Senart, date not given

"Automne". Paroles de F. Brethous-Lafargue. Chant et piano: éditions Maurice Senart 1926

"Evocation, pour Violoncello et Piano": éditions Maurice Senart 1927

"Rêve Basque." Paroles de F. Brethous-Lafargue. Chant et piano: éditions Maurice Senart 1926

"Sonata pour violoncello et piano": éditions Maurice Senart 1925

"Tourmente". Poésie de F. D'Avilla, chant et piano: éditions Maurice Senart 1928

Appendix 9: More Musical Compositions

"Chants des flots, pour chant et piano". Poésie de Fabienne Brethous-Lafargue: éditions Maurice Senart 1925

"Effeuillement, pour chant et piano". Poésie de Fabienne Brethous-Lafargue: éditions Maurice Senart 1925

"Karma, ballade pour piano": éditions Maurice Senart 1925

"Trois mélodies pour une voix, avec accompagnment de piano". J. Hamelle Editeur 1925. Pub. Maurice Senart, 1925, Paris. Bibliothèque Nationale de France

"Tes yeux verts", poésie de Albert Samain (1858–1900)

"Octobre", poésie de Fabienne Brethous-Lafargue

"Heures d'été", poésie de Albert Samain (1858–1900)

"Appel la forêt", pour chant et piano. Poésie de Fabienne Brethous-Lafargue: M. Senart 1925

"Quintette pour deux violons, alto, violoncelle et piano" Maurice Senart, Paris 1929. Held at Bibliothèque nationale de France

Thanks to Toupie Lowther Press Cuttings. Housed at The Fencing Museum.

There may well be more of her works scattered around the world: for example, Piano. Pub. Maurice Senart, Paris 1929 is also held at New York Public Library (microfilm) as well as the University of Illinois at Urbana-Champaign (microfilm).

Appendix 10

REFERENCES –
AND OTHER ITEMS OF INTEREST

Baker, Michael, *Our Three Selves, A Life of Radclyffe Hall* (Hamish Hamilton: London, 1985)

Baronova, Irina, *Irina, Ballet Life and Love* (Penguin Group: Camberwell, Australia, 2005)

Chatenay, Victor, *Mon Journal de Quatorze–Dix-Huit* (Angers, 1968)

Cline, Sally, *Radclyffe Hall: A Woman Called John* (Faber & Faber: London, 1997)

Crofton, Eileen, *The Women of Royaumont, A Scottish Women's Hospital on the Western Front* (Tuckwell Press: Edinburgh, 1997)

Daniels, Stephanie and Tedder, Anita, *A Proper Spectacle, Women Olympians 1900–1936* (ZeNaNa Press: Bedfordshire & Walla Walla Press: Australia, 2000)

Debrett's *Peerage*, Baronetage, Knightage, & Companionage 1951 (Odhams Press: London, 1950)

de Courcy, Anne, *Society's Queen. The Life of Edith Marchioness of Londonderry* (Phoenix: London, 2004)

de Goudourville, Henri, *Escrimeurs Contemporains* (Editions Chamuel: Paris, 1899. University of Alberta (Online)

de Medrano, Ricardo, *Mateos Sáinz Eulalia de Borbón: L'Enfant

Appendix 10: References – and Other Items of Interest

Terrible (Alberdi Servicios de Communicacion Avda: Spain, 2014)

Dexter, Mary, *In the Soldier's Service* (Houghton Mifflin: Boston and New York, 1918)

Dickson, Lovat, *Radclyffe Hall at the Well of Loneliness, A Sapphic Chronicle* (William Collins, Sons & Co Ltd: London and Toronto, 1975)

Doan, Laura, *Fashioning Sapphism: The Origins of a Modern English Lesbian Culture* (Columbia University Press: New York, 2001)

Doherty, R. F. and Doherty, H. L., *Lawn Tennis*. (The Baker & Taylor Company: New York, 1903, online from the Library of Congress)

Gillmeister, Heiner, *Tennis, A Cultural History* (Leicester University Press: London, 1998)

Hall, Radclyffe, *The Well of Loneliness* (Jonathan Cape: London, 1928)

Helm, Sarah, *If This is A Woman, Inside Ravensbrück* (Little, Brown: London, 2015)

Hillyard, G. W., *Forty Years of First Class Tennis* (Williams and Norgate: London, 1924) Hodges, Katherine "Memorial" unpublished. Held at Leeds University Russian Section

Kahan, Sylva, *Music's Modern Muse. A Life of Winnaretta Singer, Princesse de Polignac* (University of Rochester Press: Rochester, NY, 2003)

Lambert Chambers, Mrs Dorothy, *Lawn Tennis for Ladies* (1910, Project Gutenberg)

Marchesi, Mathilde Marchesi and Music (republished General Books, LLC: Memphis, Tenn., 2012)

McCrone, Kathleen E., *Playing the Game, Sport and the Physical Emancipation of English Women 1870–1914* (The University Press of Kentucky: Lexington, Ky, 1988)

Money, James, *Capri – Island of Pleasure* (Hamish Hamilton: London, 1986)

Myers, Wallis (ed.), *Lawn Tennis at Home and Abroad* (Charles Scribner's Sons: New York, 1904)

Ormrod, Richard, *Una Troubridge: The Friend of Radclyffe Hall*, Carroll & Graf: New York, 1985)

Tarran, Bruce, *George Hillyard, The Man Who Moved Wimbledon* (Matador: Leciester, 2013)

The Lady, "Should Women Fence" a feature for the Lady Debating Society, 30 November 1899

The Marchioness of Londonderry Retrospect (Frederick Muller Ltd.: London, 1938)

The National Archives "Fabienne Laura Evelyn Caroline Brethous-Lafargue D'Avilla" and "Memorial of Lieut. F W Lowther RN".

Souhami, Diana The Trials of Radclyffe Hall (Weidenfeld & Nicolson: London, 1998)

Una, Lady Troubridge, *The Life of Radclyffe Hall* (The Citadel Press: New York, 1963)

Thanks to the Staff of:

The British Library
The Imperial War Museum
Leeds Library
The Lonsdale Archive at Cumbria County Council Historical Research
The Motorcycle Magazine 1902 – 1962
The National Portrait Gallery
The Times Archive

Appendix 10: References – and Other Items of Interest

Thanks and Acknowledgements

Thanks also to: Father Peter from St Antony & St George Church in Duncton, West Sussex Services and the music archivist in particular; Maria Fernanda Botero from Brighton University; Marc Sena Carrel; Rosie Chassaud, for her kind help with my French; Mme Veronique Chatenay-Dolto; Professor Laura Doan from Manchester University; Malcolm Fare from the National Fencing Museum: Stella Ellis, from Pulborough; Ros Escott, for information and photos of her great aunt Nellie Rowe; Susan Harland and Shirley Carr, for the photographs of their great aunt Mlle Gabrielle de Montgeon; Paul and Su Handford; Janet Hurst from Goring-on-Thames; Lord Henley of Scaleby; the members of the Tennis Forum and the Tennis Warehouse both online; Dr Stewart Kempsell; the Squire de Lisle of Quenby Hall; Mr and Mrs Quested, from Pulborough; Mr. and Mrs. E. D. Thornton from Pulborough; Susan and Sharon; The Viscount Ullswater; Jonathan Young.

With special thanks for personal help, support, advice and patience over the years to Hilary Anderson, Diana Nichols, Marion Prince, Dr Jennifer Painter, Charlotte Ridings and the late Elaine O'Neill.

And extra special thanks to Dr Jane Traies, Sussex University, for her generous help and seemingly limitless patience and good humour.

If anyone has been missed out, multiple apologies, and please do consider yourself to be very much thanked.

Appendix 11

"Le Salon de l'Amazone"

Natalie Barney had great fun, not exactly keeping a list of the guests at her "Salon", but adding names of friends and visitors to a hand-written map of an unknown date, but probably sometime in the 1920s. The "map" shows a river, "l'Amazone", meandering out of nowhere, whisking around the garden and a vaguely octagonal central tea-table, complete with cups, saucers and a solitary tea pot, and a sideboard of fancy afternoon edibles, ending up, or possibly starting its course, at the steps of the pillared Temple of Amitié. Friendship. The names of the guests – there are over 200 – are cramped and somewhat ill written, but include everyone who was anyone in the field of the Arts, during and sometime after the turn of the century.

"T. Lowther" appears in the top left-hand corner and is surrounded by musicians. Armande de Polignac is above, and a Calvé is on the right, who can only be Emma Calvé (1858–1942), the opera singer who was the first to sing Bizet's *Carmen*. Above are Florent Schmitt (1870–1958) the composer, and below Virgil Thompson (1896–1989), also a composer. Also included on the map are many other names that will be familiar: Lady Troubridge and Radcliffe Hall feature in the

Appendix 11: "Le Salon De L'Amazone"

lower left-hand corner, their names written upside down but clearly visible.

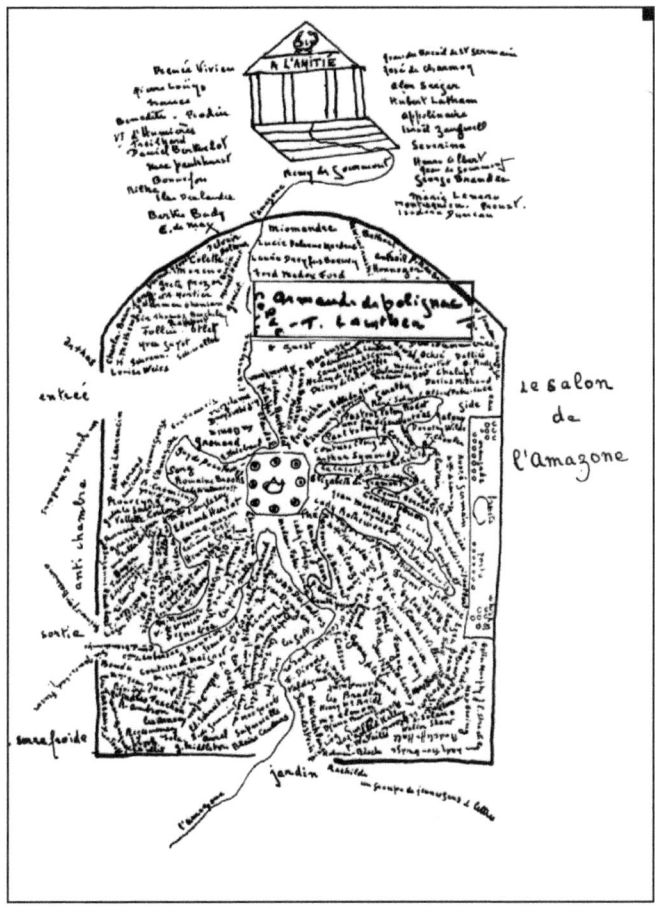

The image is reproduced here with thanks to Beinike Rare Book & Manuscripts Library, Yale University, USA and can be readily seen online.

Sources and Thanks

Inter alia...

Books and Biographies

A Gallery of her Own: An Annotated Bibliography of Women in Victorian Painting by Elree I. Harris and Shirley R. Scott : Garland Publishing Inc., 1997

A Proper Spectacle: Women Olympians 1900–1936 by Stephanie Daniels and Anita Tedder: ZeNaNA press Press, 2000

Between Me and Life: a Biography of Romaine Brooks, by Meryl Secrest: Macdonald and Jane's, 1976)

Blood and Honor, The Foreworld Graphic Novels Saga *Suffrajitsu - Mrs Pankhurst's Amazons* by Tony Wolf and Joao Viera. Pub. Foreworld, LLC, USA. 2015

Changing the Score by Hilary Poriss: Oxford University Press, 2009

Charles Meryon, A Life by Roger Collins pub. Garton & Co, Devises 1999

Daisy in Exile: The Diary of an Australian Schoolgirl in France 1887–1889 by Marc Serge Rivière: Pub. National Library of Australia, Canberra 2003

Escrimeurs Contemporains by Henry de Goudourville: Paris 1899

Sources and Thanks

Eulalia de Borbón: L'Enfant Terrible by Ricardo Mateos Sáinz de Medrano (Alberdi Servicios de Communicacion Avda, 2014

Forty Years of First Class Lawn Tennis by G. W. Hillyard: William & Norgate Ltd, 1924

George Hillyard, The Man Who Moved Wimbledon by Bruce Tarran: Matador 2013

If This is a Woman – Inside Ravensbrück: Hitler's Concentration Camp for Women by Sarah Helm: Little Brown 2015

In the Soldier's Service, War Experiences – England, Belgium, France by Mary Dexter & edited by her Mother: Houghton Mifflin Company, The Riverside Press, Cambridge, USA 1918

Irina, Ballet Life and Love by Irina Baronova: Penguin Group Australia, 2005

Jiujitsu and Judo: the Japanese Art of Self Defence from a British Athletic Point of View by Edward Barton Wright: February 1901, publisher unknown

Lawn Tennis at Home and Abroad edited by Wallis Myers New York, 1903

Lawn Tennis for Ladies by Dorothea Chambers: Methuen & Co., 1910; now available from Dodo Press USA.

L'Escrime et le tir: revue illustrée du monde des armes, online, October 1923

Marchesi and Music: Passages from the Life of a Famous Singing Teacher. New York; London: Harper & Bros. Publishers, 1898

Memories of a Doctor in War and Peace by Isabel Hutton, CBE, MD: Heinemann 1960

Mon journal de Quatorze–Dix-huit Victor Chatenay. L'Imprimerie de L'Anjou 1968

Mon Journal du Temps du Malheur Victor Chatenay: Editions du Courrier de L'Ouest, 1967

Olivia by Olivia. Hogarth Press 1949

Our Three Selves by Michael Baker pub.Hamish Hamilton, 1985

Portrait of a Seductress, The World of Natalie Barney by Jean Chalon: English translation by Crown Publishers Inc 1979

Playing the Game: Sport and the Physical Emancipation of English Women 1870–1914 by Kathleen E. McCrone (University Press of Kentucky, 1988)

Radclyffe Hall, A Woman called John by Sally Cline, Faber & Faber, 1997

Tennis, a Cultural History by Heiner Gillmeister. Leicester University Press, 1997

The Life of Radclyffe Hall by Una, Lady Troubridge 1945. Pub. the Citadel Press, New York 1961

The Lowther Family by Hugh Owen: Phillimore, 1990

The Story of My Life by Ellen Terry with Illustrations: Hutchinson & Co., 1908

The Trials of Radclyffe Hall by Diana Souhami: Weidenfeld and Nicolson, 1998

The Well of Loneliness by Radclyffe Hall: Jonathan Cape 1928

The Work of the Women's Emergency Corps in France 1915–1919, compiled by Josephine Davies

Archives, Magazines, Newspapers etc.

Country Life Magazine
HM Courts and Tribunals Service
Punch Magazine
The Cumbria Archive
The Badminton Magazine
The British Library
The British Newspaper Archive online
The Cumbria Museum of Military Life
The Lady Magazine

Sources and Thanks

The New York Times
The Newspaper Archive online
The Sketch Newspaper
The Sphere Magazine
The Sussex County Magazine
The Tatler Magazine
The Tennis Forum online
The Tennis Ware-house Online
The Times Newspaper

And the many other long departed magazines and newspapers alongside the great and seemingly endless work of The National Archives.

With special thanks to Mme Veronique Chatenay-Dolto and all the other authors, biographers, journalists, magazines, not to say the many friends from around the world whose recollections and suggestions I have quoted.